# TUDOR SCHOOL-BOY LIFE

*Juan Luis Vives.*

# TUDOR SCHOOL-BOY LIFE

The Dialogues of
JUAN LUIS VIVES

Translated into English and with an Introduction
by
FOSTER WATSON

FRANK CASS & CO. LTD
1970

Published by
FRANK CASS AND COMPANY LIMITED
67 Great Russell Street, London WC1B 3BT
by arrangement with J. M. Dent & Sons Ltd.


First edition                1908
New impression               1970


ISBN 0 7146 2279 6

*Printed in Great Britain by Clarke, Doble & Brendon Ltd.*
*Plymouth and London*

# CONTENTS

# INTRODUCTION

## J. L. VIVES: A SCHOLAR OF THE RENASCENCE

### 1492–1540

ERASMUS was born in 1466, Budé (Budaeus) in 1468, and Vives in 1492. These great men were regarded by their contemporaries as a triumvirate of leaders of the Renascence movement, at any rate outside of Italy. The name of Erasmus is now the most generally known of the three, but in one of his letters Erasmus stated his fear that he would be eclipsed by Vives. No doubt Erasmus was the greatest propagandist of Renascence ideas and the Renascence spirit. No doubt Budé, by his *Commentarii Linguae Graecae* (1529), established himself as the greatest Greek scholar of the age, Equally, without doubt, it would appear to those who have studied the educational writings of Erasmus, Budé, and Vives, the claim might reasonably be entered for J. L. Vives that his *De Tradendis Disciplinis* placed him first of the three as a writer on educational theory and practice. In 1539 Vives published at Paris the *Linguae Latinae Exercitatio, i.e.,* the *School Dialogues* which are for the first time, in the present volume, presented to the English reader.

Juan Luis Vives was born, March 6, 1492 (the year of Columbus's discovery of America), at Valencia, in Spain. His father was Luis Vives, of high-born ancestry, whose device was *Siempre vivas*. Similarly his mother, Blanca March, was of a good family, which had produced several poets. Vives himself has described his parents, their relation to each other and to himself, in two passages in his *De Institutione Feminae Christianae* (1523). This work was translated into English (*c.* 1540) by Richard Hyrde. As the two passages contain all that is known of the parents, and give a short but picturesque idea of the household relations, I transcribe them from Hyrde's translation: " My mother Blanca, when she had been fifteen years married unto my father, I could never see her strive with my father. There were two sayings that she had ever in her mouth as proverbs. When she would say she believed well anything, then she used to say, ' It is even as though Luis Vives had spoken it.' When she would say she would anything, she used to say, ' It is even as though Luis Vives would it.' I have heard my father say many times, but especially once, when one told him of a saying of Scipio African the younger, or else of Pomponius Atticus (I ween it were the saying of them both), that they never made agreement with their mothers. ' Nor I with my wife,' said he, ' which is a greater thing.' When others that heard this saying wondered upon it, and the concord of Vives and Blanca was taken up and used in a manner for a proverb, he was wont to answer like as Scipio was, who said he never made agreement with his mother, because he never made debate with her. But it is not to be much talked in a book (made for another purpose) of my most holy mother, whom I doubt not now to have in heaven the fruit and reward of her holy and pure living."

Vives states that he had the intention of writing a " book of her acts and her life," and no one who reads the foregoing passage will be otherwise than regretful that he failed to carry out this purpose. As it is, we must content ourselves with another passage.[1]

---

[1] From the same *Institution of a Christian Woman* (Richard Hyrde's translation).

" No mother loved her child better than mine did; nor any child did ever less perceive himself loved of his mother than I. She never lightly laughed upon me, she never cockered me; and yet when I had been three or four days out of her house, she wist not where, she was almost sore sick; and when I was come home, I could not perceive that ever she longed for me. Therefore there was nobody that I did more flee, or was more loath to come nigh, than my mother, when I was a child; but after I came to man's estate, there was nobody whom I delighted more to have in sight; whose memory now I have in reverence, and as oft as she cometh to my remembrance I embrace her within my mind and thought, when I cannot with my body."

Vives went to the town school of Valencia. The outlines of the history of this school have been sketched by Dr. Rudolf Heine.[1] The foundation of the school dates back to the time of James I. of Aragon, when Pope Innocent IV. gave privileges to the newly founded school in 1245. The school, Dr. Heine says, was first a *schola*, then a *studium*, then a *gymnasium*, and in the fifteenth and sixteenth centuries was known as an *academy*, the name by which Vives describes schools in the *Colloquies*. In 1499 new statutes were drawn up for the Valencia Academy, ordaining the teaching of grammar, logic, natural and moral philosophy, metaphysics, canon and civil law, poetry, and " other subjects such as the city desires and requires."

The spirit of scholasticism reigned supreme in the Valencian Academy when Vives was a pupil. The dominant subject of study was dialectic, and the all-controlling method of education was the disputation. Vives thus received a thorough drilling in dialectic and disputation. When Vives became a convert to the Renascence interest of literature and grammar,

[1] J. L. Vives: *Ausgeswählte pädagogische Schriften.* Leipzig.

he was thus well prepared by his experience in the Valencian Academy for an effective onslaught on the old disputational methods. How deeply interwoven these methods were in the school instruction may be seen in Vives' own words:—

" Even the youngest scholars (*tyrones*) are accustomed never to keep silence; they are always asserting vigorously whatever comes uppermost in their minds, lest they should seem to be giving up the dispute. Nor does one disputation or even two each day prove sufficient, as for instance at dinner. They wrangle at breakfast; they wrangle after breakfast; before supper they wrangle, and they wrangle after supper. . . . At home they dispute, out of doors they dispute. They wrangle over their food, in the bath, in the sweating-room, in the church, in the town, in the country, in public, in private; at all times they are wrangling."

The names of two of Vives' schoolmasters are preserved, Jerome Amiguetus and Daniel Siso. Amiguetus was a thorough-going scholastic, teaching by the old mediæval methods, and a stalwart opponent of the Renascence. Spain generally resisted the Revival of Learning, and wished to have a ban placed even on the works of Erasmus. But in the person of Antonio Calà Harana Del Ojo, better known as Antonio de Lebrijà (or Antonius Nebrissensis), a doughty champion of classicism appeared and raised a Spanish storm. In 1492, the year of Vives' birth, Antonio published a grammar and a dictionary, and had the hardihood to present his learning in the Spanish language. About 1506 it was proposed to introduce Antonio's *Introductiones Latinae* into the Valencian Academy. This suggestion was strenuously opposed by Amiguetus. With the enthusiasm of a school-boy of fourteen years of age, Vives espoused the side of his teacher, and by declamation and by pen supported the old methods.

But when he published his *De Tradendis Disciplinis* (1531) more than a quarter of a century afterwards, he paid Lebrijà the praise which as a school-boy he had withheld, recognising his varied and broad reading, his intimate knowledge of classical writers, his glorious scholarship, and his modesty in only claiming to be a grammarian.

Of Vives' school-life little more can be gathered, except indeed what in his writings may be surmised to be the reminiscences of his own boy-life. We find glimpses of this kind in the *Dialogues*. For example, in the twenty-second Dialogue—which expounds the laws of school games—he describes his native town and early environment.

In 1509 Vives went to Paris to continue his studies. Amongst the teachers under whom he studied here was the Spanish John Dullard. Vives tells us that Dullard used to say: Quanto eris melior grammaticus, tanto pejus dialecticus et theologus![1] Nevertheless, Paris had awakened Vives to the unsatisfactory nature of a one-sided training in dialectic. In 1512 he proceeded to Bruges. He became tutor in a Spanish family, by name Valdaura. One of the daughters, Margaret, whom he taught, he afterwards (in 1524) married. He speaks of the mother of the family, Clara Cervant, in the highest terms, and regarded her—next to his own mother—as the highest example of womanly devotion to duty he had ever known, for she had nursed her husband, it is said, from their marriage day for many years through a severe and obstinate illness. Whilst at Bruges his thoughts gathered strength in the direction of the Renascence. In 1514 he suggests that Ferdinand of Spain would do well to get Erasmus as tutor in his family, for he says Erasmus is known to him personally, and is all that is dear and worthy. It is thus certain

---

[1] *De Causis Corruptarum Artium*, book ii.

that Vives was confirmed by Erasmus in the study of classical literature as transcending all the old mediæval educational disciplines.

From 1512 onwards, with breaks, Vives' main quarters were in Flanders, at Bruges or Louvain, at the former of which was the residence of many of his Spanish compatriots. One of these breaks of residence was in 1514 at Paris, another at Lyons in 1516. In 1518 Vives was at Lyons, where he was entrusted with the education of William de Croy, Cardinal designate and Archbishop of Toledo. The course of instruction which he gave was founded on a thorough reading of the ancient authors and instruction in rhetoric and philosophy. At Lyons, too, Vives met Erasmus. " Here we have with us," writes Erasmus in one of his letters, " Luis Vives, who has not passed his twenty-sixth year of age. Young as he is, there is no part of philosophy in which he does not possess a knowledge which far outstrips the mass of students. His power of expression in speech and writing is such as I do not know any one who can be declared his equal at the present time." In 1519 Vives was at Paris, where he became personally acquainted with the great William Budé. Of him Vives, in one of his letters to Erasmus, writes, " What a man ! One is astounded at him whether we consider his knowledge, his character, or his good fortune." But more interesting to English readers, is a letter about this time (1519) of Sir Thomas More on seeing some of the published work of Vives himself. He says: " Certainly, my dear Erasmus, I am ashamed of myself and my friends, who take credit to ourselves for a few brochures of a quite insignificant kind, when I see a young man like Vives producing so many well-digested works, in a good style, giving proof of an exquisite erudition. How great is his knowledge of Greek and Latin; greater still is the way in which he is versed in branches of knowledge

of the first rank. Who in this respect is there who surpasses
Vives in the quantity and depth of his knowledge? But
what is most admirable of all is that he should have acquired
all this knowledge so as to be able to communicate it to
others by instruction. For who instructs more clearly, more
agreeably, or more successfully than Vives?"

At this point may be stated the chief works which Vives so
far had written:—

1570. The boyish *Declamationes in Antonium Nebrissensem* (not extant).

1509. *Veritas Fucata*, in which he designates the contents of the
classics as "food for demons."

1514. *Jesu Christi Triumphus.*

1518. *De Initiis, Sectis et Laudibus Philosophiae*, perhaps the first
modern work on the history of philosophy.

1519. *In Pseudo-dialecticos.* This famous treatise pours its invective
and indignation against the formalistic disputational dialectic of
the schools of Paris, and marks Vives' complete break with scholastic mediævalism, and his acceptance of the Renascence material
of knowledge and methods of inquiry.

1519. *Pompeius Fugiens.*

1519. *Praelectio in Quartum Rhetoricorum in Herensium.*

1519. The Dialogue called *Sapiens.*

1519. *Praelectio in Convivia Phillipi.*

1519. *Censura de Aristotelis Operibus.*

1519. Edited *Somnium Scipionis*, the introduction to which was afterwards known as *Somnium Vivis*. Vives here regards Plato as the
herald of Christianity.

1520. *Sex Declamationes.*

1520. *Aedes Legum.* In this book Vives made important suggestions
founded on Roman law for the improvement of law in his own
times.

At the beginning of 1521 Vives' old pupil and patron,
Cardinal de Croy, died. It was at this time he took in hand
his great work, the commentary on St. Augustine's *Civitas Dei.*
Erasmus suggested the work to him, so that Vives might do
for St. Augustine what Erasmus himself had done for the
works of St. Jerome. Vives' edition of St. Augustine's
*Civitas Dei* was dedicated to King Henry VIII. of England.

The writing of this commentary was a huge labour, and it
marks two crises in Vives' life—firstly, he fell ill with a
tertian fever, and, secondly, he gave up his teaching of
youths, work which he had hitherto strenuously pursued
along with his literary labours.    In 1522 he wrote a pleading
letter to Erasmus, begging him forgive his slowness in de-
spatching the *Civitas Dei*.    In it he confesses that " school-
keeping has become in the highest degree repulsive," and
that he would rather do anything else than any longer continue " *inter has sordes et pueros.*"    It appears that at the
time Vives was giving three lectures daily in the University
of Louvain as well as teaching boys.

In the autumn of 1522 Vives came to England for a short
visit, and in the following year he was offered the Readership
in Humanity in the University of Oxford.    Whilst at Oxford
he lived in Corpus Christi College.    He had for patron Queen
Catharine of Aragon, to whom he dedicated his *De Institutione Feminae Christianae*, which was published in 1523.
Vives was entrusted with the direction of the Princess Mary
(afterwards Queen Mary I.), for whose use was written *De
Ratione Studii Puerilis ad Catharinam Reginam Angliae*, 1523.
In the same year Vives also wrote *De Ratione Studii Puerilis
ad Carolum Montjoium Guilielmi Filium*.    These two trac-
tates present an excellent account of the best Renascence
views on education, in Tudor times, of a girl and a boy
respectively.

The *De Institutione Feminae Christianae* already mentioned
is one of the earliest and most important Tudor documents
on women's education.    It marks the transition from the old
mediæval tradition of the cloistral life as the highest womanly
ideal to that of training for domestic life, in which the mother
should be distinguished by the deepest culture of piety and
all the intellectual education conducive to religious develop-

ment.  It may be described as typical of Catholic Puritanism in the education of women in the Tudor times.

From 1522 onwards, till after the divorce of Catharine of Aragon, Vives appears to have spent a portion of the year in England, and to have earned enough money to keep him for the rest of the year in Flanders or elsewhere, where he continued his literary career.  Although he sometimes lectured in Oxford his time seems principally to have been spent at the court of Henry VIII. and his wife, Catharine.  He had times of great weariness in England.  He writes in one of his letters of his London life: " I have as sleeping place a narrow den, in which there is no chair, no table.  Around it are the quarters of others, in which so constant and great noise prevails that it is impossible to settle one's mind to anything, however much one may have the will or need. In addition, I live a distance from the royal palace, and in order not to lose the whole day by often going and coming back, from early morning till late evening I have no time at home.  When I have taken my mid-day meal I cannot once turn round in my narrow and low room, but must waltz round and round as on a cheese.  Study is out of the question in such circumstances.  I have to take great care of my health, for if I became ill they would cast me like a mangy dog on a dung-hill.  Whilst eating I read, but I eat little, for with so much sitting I cannot digest, as I should do if I walked about.  For the rest, life here is such that I cannot hide my ennui.  About the only thing I can do, is to do nothing."

Vives enjoyed allowances both from the king and from the queen, and he had other sources of earnings.  In 1524 he was back in Flanders to marry his pupil Margaret Valdaura.  Soon after his marriage, which appears to have been a very happy one—though with Vives' frequent travelling the two were often separated—he wrote one of his widest circulated works, the *Introductio ad Sapientiam,* which presents the grounds of the Christian religion and the right fashioning of life by intelligence and temperance.

Vives next turned his attention to great European military contests, and was a warm advocate of international peace between Christian powers together with combined warfare against the Turks. These views he elaborated in 1526 in his *De Europae Dissidiis et Bello Turico.* More remarkable still, in the same year, was his treatise, *De Subventione Pauperum,* in which he is the first advocate of national state provision for the poor. He would require those who are poor by their own fault to submit to compulsory labour, and even to help in the provision for other poor people.

In 1528 Vives wrote his *De Officio Mariti,* a companion volume to the *De Institutione Feminae Christianae.* In this year he had to leave England for good, since Henry VIII. was determined to divorce Catharine of Aragon. Vives was a strong supporter of Catharine. It is said that the queen wished to have Vives as her counsel before the judges on the case, but Henry cast Vives in prison for six weeks, and only freed him on the condition that he left the court and England. Vives retreated to Belgium.

In 1529 Vives wrote the *De Concordia et Discordia in Humano Genero,* another large-hearted discourse on the value of peace. In 1531 appeared his great pædagogical work, the *De Disciplinis.*[1] In 1539 he wrote the *De Anima et Vita,* one of the first modern works on psychology, and the *De Veritate Fidei Christianae.* And in the same year appeared the *Linguae Latinae Exercitatio* or the *School Dialogues.* Vives died May 6, 1540.

[1] The *De Disciplinis* consists of two parts—1. *De Causis Corruptarum Artium,* in seven books; 2. *De Tradendis Disciplinis* in five books.

The *De Disciplinis,* with the two divisions *De Causis Corruptarum Artium* and the *De Tradendis Disciplinis,* and the *Exercitatio* are the great pædagogical works of Vives, the first a most comprehensive theoretical work of education, probably the greatest Renascence book on education. The *Exercitatio* is perhaps the most interesting school-text-book of the age.

# THE SIGNIFICANCE OF THE *DIALOGUES* OF
# J. L. VIVES

## The Poverty of the Vernacular Literature before the Tudor Period

It is difficult to realise the position of the student of literature in England in the first half of the sixteenth century. The whole wealth of the Elizabethan writers, and all their successors in the Ages of Milton, of Dryden and Pope, of Samuel Johnson, of Charles Lamb, of Shelley, Byron, and Wordsworth, and the large range of Victorian literature, all this had to come. The modern man, therefore, must confess that it was not to English literature that the Tudor student could look for the material of education. Even if it be justifiable to claim that modern literature is a more fruitful study than ancient literature, for the ordinary man, the question remains: How was the ordinary educated man to be trained in the earlier Tudor Age, when the time of great modern literature was " not yet "?

Before we can understand the function served by a Latin text-book of boys' dialogues like the work of Vives translated in this volume, we must, therefore, first realise the poverty of the vernacular literature of periods anterior to the sixteenth century, and the consequent delight of scholars in finding Latin and Greek literature ready to hand.

" There is every reason to believe that the English language, before the invention of printing, was held by learned or literary men in very little esteem. In the library of Glastonbury Abbey, which bids fair to have been one of the most extensive in the kingdom in 1248, there were but four books in English, and those upon religious subjects, all beside *vetusta et inutilia.* We have not a single historian in English prose before the reign of Richard II., when John Trevisa translated the *Polychronicon* of Randulph Higden. Boston of Bury, who seems to have consulted all the monasteries in England, does not mention one author who had written in English; and Bale, at a later period, has comparatively but an insignificant number; nor was Leland so fortunate as to find above two or three English books in the monastic and other libraries which he rummaged and explored under the King's Commission." [1]

The classical writers of Greece and Rome, however, have always drawn towards them a large proportion of the well-trained scholarly men of each generation. *Before the vernacular literature existed, necessarily it was to the ancient classical languages that the literary scholar turned.* In Greek, Plato and Aristotle had written; so, too, Aeschylus, Sophocles, Euripides, as dramatists, and the historians Thucydides, Herodotus, Xenophon, and the "divine poet" Homer. Amongst the Latin prose writers were Cicero, Terence, Livy; and amongst the poets, Horace and Vergil. On any showing, such classical writers hold their own high place even if brought into comparison with the greatest of the moderns. The intellectual discipline received by reading their works in the original Greek and Latin had its value. Hence the sixteenth-century English student was trained on those ancient Greek and Latin authors, all unconscious of the great awakening that was to be of modern English literature, into which the twentieth-century reader so lightly enters.

The whole of the well-educated, scholarly, learned men of the sixteenth century, in England and on the continent of

[1] *Dissertation on Romance and Minstrelsy,* by Joseph Ritson, 1891.

Europe, all entered into the *same* classical heritage. They all honoured the same great names of Greek and Latin authors. Latin was the learned language, as the language of Latin literature, as well as the starting-point for the study of Greek. Latin, too, was spoken in every country amongst the learned, and even amongst many who were not regarded as learned. Latin was, it is to be clearly understood, not only a dead language, but a current, live language. It is said that beggars begged in Latin; shopkeepers and innkeepers, and indeed all who had to deal with the general public of travellers, are credited with a knowledge of some colloquial Latin. Church services, of course, were all in Latin, and youths were taught for the most part in the chantries of the churches, and even elementary education provided sufficient knowledge of Latin to enable the pupil to help the priest to say mass, *i.e.*, a minimum of Latin and of music.

Latin, therefore, at least occupied the place in the Mediæval Ages which French holds to-day as an international language. When Laurentius Valla, about 1440, wrote his epoch-making *Elegantiae Latinae Linguae*, his aim was not to induce people to speak Latin—all well-conducted persons, of course, did so—but to give them the facilities for speaking *correct and well-chosen* Latin phrases, such as Cicero or Terence would have used. The complaint of the writers of the Renascence times was not that students and the ordinary educated people did not speak Latin, but that they spoke it so inaccurately that the Latin was spoken differently, not only in pronunciation but also in construction, in different countries, and even in different parts of the same country. Text-book after text-book was written to expose and correct the barbarisms in Latin which had become current. For this reason, in our own country, Dean Colet enjoined the reading of good litera-ture in Latin and Greek. Colet requires " that filthiness and all such abusion which the later blind world brought in, which much rather may be called blotterature than literature," shall be absent from the famous school of St. Paul's, which he founded.

The Renascence influence, then, attempted on the educational side to bring the pupils of the schools away from the jargon and barbarism of current Latin to the classical Latin of Terence and Cicero. The Renascence leaders had the courage to hope to bring this reform even into the ordinary conversation of educated men and women in their speaking of Latin.

Into this aim Vives entered with the keenest enthusiasm. This will become evident by reference to the Dedication of the *Dialogues* which I give in full.

### THE DEDICATION OF THE SCHOOL-DIALOGUES OF VIVES:

" Vives to Philip, son and heir to the august Emperor Charles, with all good will.

" Very great are the uses of the Latin language both for speaking and thinking rightly. For that language is as it were the treasure-house of all erudition, since men of great and outstanding minds have written on every branch of knowledge in the Latin speech. Nor can any one attain to the knowledge of these subjects except by first learning Latin. For which reason I shall not grudge, though engaged in the pursuit of higher researches, to set myself to help forward to some degree the elementary studies of youth. I have, in these Dialogues, written a first book of practice in speaking the Latin language as suitable as possible, I trust, to boys. It has seemed well to dedicate it to thee, Boy-Prince, both because of thy father's goodwill to me, in the highest degree, and also because I shall deserve well of my country, that is, Spain, if I should help in the forming of sound morals in thy mind. For our country's health is centred in thy soundness and wisdom. But thou wilt hear more fully and often enough on these matters from John Martinius Siliceus, thy teacher."

It will be noted that the expressed aim of Vives is to help boys *who are learning to speak the Latin language.* For this purpose, Vives realised that the method must be conversational, that the style of speech must be clear, correct, and as far as possible based on classical models, and that the subject-matter must consist of topics interesting to children and connected with their daily life. The Prince Philip, to whom the Dialogues are dedicated, it should be noted, was afterwards Philip II., the consort of the English Queen Mary I., daughter of Catharine of Aragon.

## Contents of the Dialogues

The German historian of Latin School - Dialogues, Dr. Bömer, speaks of the characteristic power of Vives in introducing, in relatively short space, the ordinary daily life of boys, and tracking it into the smallest corners. "If a boy is putting on his clothes, we learn every single article of clothing, and all the topics of toilettes and the names of each object (Dialogues I. and XI.). When two school-boys pay a visit to a stranger's house, we have shown to us its whole inner arrangement by an expert guide (XII.). Interesting observations are made on the different parts of the human body by a painter, Albert Dürer (XXIII.). With a banquet as the occasion, we are introduced to the equipment of a dining-room (XVI.), with ordinary kinds of foods and drinks (XVII.), and if we like we can betake ourselves to the cook in the kitchen and watch the direction of operations (XV.).

We are told in another Dialogue (XVIII.) of a man's fear to go home to his wife after too liberal a banquet, and how she would entertain him with longer homilies than those of St. Chrysostom. When a company of scholars wish to make a distant excursion, all kinds of horses and carriages, with their trappings, are presented to the notice of the reader (IX.)." [1] Then, to show us life under the most favourable of circumstances, Vives gives a dialogue on the King's Palace (XIX.).

Whilst the general environments of boys' lives are thus pourtrayed in considerable detail, Vives is particularly careful to show boys the general features and significance of home and school life, and regards it as part of his duty to expound, in the last two dialogues, some general guiding principles of education for the boys, their teachers, and readers of the book to ponder over.

## HOME AND SCHOOL LIFE

The first dialogue treats of getting up in the morning. The girl Beatrice tries to rouse the two boys Emanuel and Eusebius, the latter of whom makes the excuse, " I seem to have my eyes full of sand," to which Beatrice replies, " That is always your morning song." Then the boys dress. Beatrice enjoins them, " Kneel down before this image of our Saviour and say the Lord's Prayer, etc. Take care, my Emanuel, that you think of nothing else while you are praying." The interchange of wit between the boys and the maid is an interesting picture of child-life. In the second dialogue, after family morning greetings, which include playing with the little dog Ruscio, the father teaches his

[1] Bömer, *Die Lateinischen Schulergespräche der Humanisten* (1899) p. 182.

little boy the difference between the little dog and a little boy. "What have you," he asks his child, "in you why you should become a man and not he?" He suggests to him that the difference really is contained in the magic word "school." The boy says: "I will go, father, with all the pleasure in the world." Whereupon the boy's elder sister gets him his little satchel and puts him up his breakfast (*i.e.*, lunch) in it. The father takes the boy to the school, and (in III.) discusses with a neighbour the comparative merits of the schoolmasters Varro and Philoponus. The father is told that Philoponus has the *smaller* number of boys, and at once decides: "I should prefer him!" Then as Philoponus comes into view, he turns to his boy, saying: "Son, this is as it were the laboratory for the formation of men, and Philoponus is the artist-educator. Christ be with you, Master! Uncover your head, my boy, and bow your right knee. . . . Now stand up!"

*Philoponus.* May your coming to us be a blessing to all! What may be your business?

*Father.* I bring you this boy of mine for you to make of him a man from the beast.

*Philoponus.* This shall be my earnest endeavour. He shall become a man from the beast, a fruitful and good creature out of a useless one. Of that have no doubt.

*Father.* What is the charge for the instruction you give?

*Philoponus.* If the boy makes good progress it will be little; if not, a good deal.

*Father.* That is acutely and wisely said, as is all you say. We share the responsibility then; you to instruct zealously, I to recompense your labour richly.

It will thus be seen that the idea of co-operation and consultation of parents and teachers is no new one.[1] But the enthusiasm of the parent, depicted by Vives, to recompense

[1] Vives deals with this question in his *De Tradendis Disciplinis*, and it is highly probable that Mulcaster had read that book before he treated on the subject of conferences of parents and teachers. (*Positions*, p. 284).

the teacher "richly" can hardly be said to have continued, if it existed in the Tudor age, outside of Vives' generous heart.

The next dialogue (IV.) shows how boys loitered on the way to school, their difference in powers, and in the practice of observations and the self-training of the senses and wits in the streets, such as made R. L. Stevenson wonder if the truant from school did not gain more by his self-chosen though casual wanderings than if he had gone orderly to school.

An account of actual school-work in the subjects of reading (V.) and writing (X.) is given, and the *raison d'être* of school instruction in these subjects suggested. The boys go home (VI.) and a most pleasing picture is given of home-life, with the mother, the boys, the girls, and the serving maiden, introducing children's games and the interference of meals with games.

Dialogue VII. deals with school-meals, and we plunge at once right into the heart of school interests and life. The sort of foods and drinks, the different kinds of banquets and feastings, mentioned in older writers, the preparation of the table, moderation in eating and drinking, the necessity of cleanliness in all the stages of a meal, including washing up, become topics of the dialogue as it proceeds. Then comes the fitting device of introducing a guest to the boys' table, of another boy, a Fleming from Bruges. He is asked if he has brought his knife. He has not. "This is a wonder!" exclaims an interlocutor. "A Fleming without a knife, and he too a Brugensian, where the best knives are made!" The conversation proceeds *in Latin*, since boys were required to speak *in and out* of school in Latin, at least in all self-respecting establishments.

The Brugensian boy has been under John Theodore Nervius, and this becomes the occasion for a compliment to that schoolmaster. Bruges, too, we have seen, was the

town in which Vives himself spent a considerable portion
of his adult life. He does not hesitate to introduce himself,
humorously, into this dialogue on school-boys' meals.

*Master.* But what is our Vives doing?
*Nepotulus.* They say he is in training as an athlete, but not by athletics.
*Master.* What is the meaning of that?
*Nepotulus.* He is always wrestling, but not bravely enough.
*Master.* With whom?
*Nepotulus.* With his *gout*.
*Master.* O mournful wrestler, which first of all attacks the feet.
*Usher.* Nay, rather cruel victor, which fetters the whole body!

In this dialogue of school-boy meals, Vives has given
samples of conversational topics, and their due treatment,
in the presence of masters and in regular daily routine. In
the next dialogue (VIII.), called " Pupils' Chatter," boys are
out of doors, and a series of nineteen "stories" or topics of
conversation get started. The subjects are of interest in
showing the type of incidents which boys were supposed to
introduce into conversation, and though didactic in tendency,
certainly do not favour the supposition that school-boys were
supposed to be absorbed in the study of recondite classical
subtleties, or even in purely Ciceronian subjects.

Dialogue IX., " Journey on Horseback," contains the
record of what modern educationalists call "the school
journey." The idea of studying geography and history by
taking journeys, in which instruction shall arise naturally
out of the places of interest seen in the course of the journey,
is not a new one, as is often supposed. Vittorino da Feltre,
for instance, used to take his school in the summer months
for excursions from Mantua to Goito. Vives represents his
Parisian pupil as journeying from Paris to Boulogne. The
occasion of holiday for the pupils is that Pandulphus, their
teacher, has "incepted" in the university, and having thus
become a " Master of Arts " (with the right to teach school

on his own account), according to university custom he is performing his duty of giving a great feast to the other masters in honour of his laurels, and as a matter of fact, as these boys recognise, is making them drunk. This dialogue of the " Journey on Horseback " contains a full account of different kinds of locomotion. It is especially distinguished by the love that is shown for natural objects of the country, the river, the sweet scent of the fields, the nightingale, and the goldfinch.

In Dialogue XIII. the school is described. Each type and grade of scholar is discussed. Vives' conception of a school was afterwards followed by Milton. It was an academy, in which the pupil remained from early years up to and including the university stage. In this dialogue is the account of a disputation, with description of the *propugnator* of a thesis, and several types of oppugnators.

Dialogue XIV. describes a scholar burning the midnight oil. Vives describes the extensive preparations of the scholar for his work of reading authors. The account is almost a supplement to Erasmus's famous picture of the Ciceronian scholar setting himself to his composition. The dialogue ends with the scholar going to bed whilst one of his attendants sings to the accompaniment of the lyre the lines of Ovid beginning: *Somne, quies rerum, placidissime somne deorum.*

It has already been stated that Vives devoted a dialogue to an account of the King's Palace. Similarly, in speaking now of Vives' treatment of school life, careful notice should be taken of the fact that one dialogue (XX.) is concerned with the education of the boy-prince. This dialogue is of especial interest, since the boy-prince is Philip himself, the son of the Emperor Charles V., the child to whom Vives dedicates the *Dialogues*. Philip was born at Valladolid, May 21, 1527,

and was therefore eleven years of age when Vives completed
the writing of the *Dialogues* and was twelve years old when
they appeared. It will be remembered that in 1554 Philip
came to England to claim as his bride the English Queen
Mary I., the " bloody " Mary, daughter of Catharine of
Aragon, the first queen-consort of Henry VIII., whose coming
to England was probably to some degree the ground of its
attraction to Vives when he paid his first visit to England,
in the autumn of 1522. It is interesting to note that Vives
wrote, in 1523, a short treatise on the education of the
Princess Mary, probably at the request of Queen Catharine
of Aragon, and at any rate dedicated to that ill-fated queen.
Vives, thus, is in the remarkable position of having prescribed,
as consultant-educationalist, for the Spanish Philip in one of
his dialogues (in 1538) and for the English Mary in 1523.[1]

In this dialogue, " The Boy Prince," are the interlocutors,
Prince Philip and the two counsellor-teachers, Morobulus
and Sophobulus. Morobulus is a fawning sycophant, who
advises Philip to " ride about, chat with the daughters of your
august mother, dance, learn the art of bearing arms, play
cards or ball, leap and run." But as for the study of literature, why, that is for men of " holy " affairs, priests or
artisans, who want technical knowledge. Get plenty of fresh
air. Philip replies that he cannot follow all this advice without opposing his tutors, Stunica and Siliceus. Morobulus
points out that these tutors are subjects of Philip, or at any
rate of Philip's father. Philip observes that his father has
placed them over him. Morobulus advises resistance to
them. Sophobulus urges, on the contrary, that if Philip
does not obey them, he will become a "slave of the worst

[1] It should be remembered, in connection with these dates, that
Queen Mary was eleven years older than Philip. Mary was Philip's
second wife; his first wife was Mary of Portugal, whom he married in
1543. She died in 1546.

order, worse than those who are bought and sold from Ethiopia or Africa and employed by us here." [1]

Sophobulus then shows, by three similitudes, that safety in actions and in the events of life depends upon knowledge and study. First, he proposes a game in which one is elected king. " The rest are to obey according to the rules of the game." Let Philip be king. But Philip inquires as to the nature of the game. If he does not know the game, he inquires, how can he take the part of king in it?

Secondly, Philip is invited to ride the ferocious Neapolitan steed, well known for its kicking proclivities. Eleven-year-old Philip declines, because he has not as yet learned the art of managing a refractory horse, and has not got the strength to master such a horse.

Thirdly, Philip is offered, and declines, the rôle of pilot of a boat, which has lately been overturned by an unskilled helmsman.

The young prince is thus led to recognise that for playing games rightly, for riding properly, for directing a boat safely, in all these cases adequate knowledge and skill is necessary. He himself is led to suggest (in true pedagogical method) that for governing his kingdom it will be necessary for him to acquire the knowledge of the art and skill of sound government, and that this knowledge can only be gained by assiduous study and learning. Sophobulus leads the young prince, further, to the recognition that helpful wisdom can be learned from " monitors " like Plato, Aristotle, Cicero, Seneca, Livy, Plutarch. Philip asks: " How can we learn from the dead? Can the dead speak? " " Yes," is the reply. " These very men and others like them, departed from this earth, will talk to you as often and as much as you like."

[1] *See* p. 174,

Surely Vives has chosen an attractive and reasonable way of presenting the significance of literature to the child. He uses a further illustration in urging the study of the words and writings of wise men. " Imagine that over the river yonder there was a narrow plank as bridge, and that every one told you that as many as rode on horseback and attempted thus to cross it had fallen into the water, and were in danger of their lives, and, moreover, with difficulty they had been dragged out half dead. . . . Would not, in such a case, a man seem to you to be demented, who, taking that journey, did not get off from his horse and escape from the danger in which the others had fallen? "

*Philip*. To be sure he would.
*Sophobulus*. And rightly.   Seek now from old men, as to what chiefly they have felt unfortunate in this life, what negligence in themselves they most bitterly regret.   All will answer with one voice, so far as they have learned anything, their regret is " not to have learned more."

In two points the young Prince Philip seems to have risen to meet Vives' hopes. When Philip came to England in 1554 and married Queen Mary, he is reported to have announced that he wished to live like an Englishman. He asked for beer at a public dinner, and " gravely commended it as the wine of the country." He evidently had acquired courteous bearing. Still more clearly, in accordance with the wishes expressed in the Dedication, is the statement of the fact that Philip addressed in Latin a deputation of the council which he received at Southampton, on landing, and further that it was decided that reports of proceedings of the council should be made in Latin or Spanish. Whether Philip had learned to speak Latin from Vives' *School Dialogues* is not recorded, but it is not unlikely.

The Dedication of the *Dialogues* shows how earnestly Vives had sought to influence Prince Philip. The last two dialogues (XXIV. and XXV.) endeavour to lay down sound principles of education. The boys (and Prince Philip amongst them) who had read through the preceding dialogues were not to be dismissed until Vives had declared to them the whole gospel of education, as he conceived it. Learning Latin, even to speak it eloquently and to write it accurately, is not of itself education; even to read the sayings and writings of the wise and experienced dead, and to listen to the exhortations and suggestions of the noblest and most learned of living men, is not necessarily the essence of education. The underlying impulse of the student, the roots of his will, must be taken into account. Education is not the adornment of mental distinctions for the sake of popularity or reputation. It is not the acquisition of an additional charm to a particular grade of nobility. It is no artificial appanage. It is not a class distinction. The real argument for education is that it makes a man a *better* man. If you use the word better it implies the *good*. Vives shows " the good " does not consist in riches, honours, position, or in learning merely, but in a keen intellect, wise mature judgment, religion, piety towards God, and in performance of duties towards one's country, one's dependants, one's parents, and in the cultivation of justice, temperance, liberality, magnanimity, equability of mind in calamity and brave bearing in adversity. It is in the acquisition of these qualities (for which learning is of high service) that we get " real, solid, noble education." Such training to the man of court-life will bring " true urbanity," and make him " pleasing and dear to all. But even this thou wilt not set at high value, but wilt have as sole care—to become acceptable to the Eternal God."

### Subject-matter and Style

In studying a work like the *School-boy Dialogues* of Juan Luis Vives the modern reader is likely to be attracted much more by the subject-matter than by the literary style of the author. Were the chief interest in Vives' style, it would be difficult to plead any justification for presenting an English translation. But the fact is that these *School Dialogues*, in the course of time, have become, as it were, historical documents, serving a purpose which was certainly far from being present in the mind of the author. Vives, no doubt, wished his book to be regarded as good and pure Latinity, and would have been hurt to the quick if he had been charged with the barbarisms and inaccuracies which it was the very object of the book to supplant. But as for the subject-matter, he wanted it to contain the Latin expressions for all sorts of common *things* which entered into the notice of, and required mention from, the young student of Latin. Vives is thus the forerunner of Comenius, and when he treats of subjects such as clothes, the kitchen, the bed-chamber, dining-room, papers and books, the exterior of the body of man, and supplies the Latin for all the terms used in connection with these subjects, he is exactly on Comenius's ground in the *Janua Linguorum* and the *Orbis Pictus*. But Vives is to be distinguished in two ways from Comenius:—(1) he is constantly in touch with the real interests of boys; (2) he is greatly concerned as to his methods of expression.

It is partly because Vives' *Dialogues* are intrinsically attractive that we are content to believe they are a true picture of boys' manners, habits, and life in the Tudor period. By their realistic sincerity the dialogues bring with them their own evidence of unconscious reality. But further evidence is to be found in the great success and popularity of the dialogues. For had the details been inaccurate and *invraisemblables*, and had there been a wrong emphasis of educational spirit, it is not likely that the book would have had its extensive vogue. It must be remembered that there were many competing collections of dialogues. Vives' *Dialogues* may therefore be regarded as being amongst the survivals of the fittest. Probably the Latin dialogues for schools which have actually had the widest circulation are those of Erasmus, Maturinus Corderius, and Sébastien Castellion. Of these undoubtedly the dialogues of Vives (1538) and of Corderius (whose dialogues were first published in 1564) throw the most light upon the school-life of boys and the conditions of the schools.

An amiable feature of the *School Dialogues* of Vives is the introduction, not uncommon in school dialogue-books, of well-known persons, ancient and contemporary, amongst the interlocutors. In this way Vives brings before the boys people like Prince Philip, Vitruvius, Joannes Jocundus Veronensis, and Baptista Albertus Leo, all famous architects (Vitruvius being an author of antiquity, the other two nearer Vives' time), Pliny, Epictetus, Celsus, Dydimus, Aristippus, Scopas, Polaemon, and personal friends like Valdaura (one of the Bruges family into which Vives married), Honoratus Joannius, Gonzalus Tamayus; the painter Albert Dürer, the scholar Simon Grynaeus, and the poet Caspar Velius, and the great Greek scholar and educationalist Budaeus. Vives delights in devoting one of the dialogues to describe his native town Valencia, and in introducing local references of persons and places there. He also (in Dialogue X.) refers to Antonius Nebrissensis, the first to use Spanish vernacular in connection with Latin text-books. His references to schoolmasters are very numerous, and include many types. They are probably founded upon teachers known to him.

One point further should be mentioned. Vives wishes to supply details in the richest profusion in his various subjects. if for no other reason at least so as to increase the vocabulary of the pupils. Accordingly for his subject-matter he quotes and borrows from many of the old writers. J. T. Freigius, in his Nürnberg edition of 1582, not only names the various ancient authors on technical subjects whom Vives has consulted, but also suggests further reading of authors, whom he might with advantage have also quoted. Looking on the *Dialogues* as a whole, it is remarkable that so many interests were conciliated, as if by instinct—*e.g.*, the schoolboy, the schoolmaster, the general reader, even in some cases the readers desirous of technical instruction. But the unifying factor was the desire of all those and others to learn to speak Latin, and to know the Latin terms for all useful objects.

## POPULARITY

J. T. Freigius, in the preface to his edition of 1582, tells us that the dialogues of Vives were read in his time " in well-nigh every school." Bömer quotes orders for the government of ten grammar schools in Germany, between 1564 and 1661, in which the dialogues of Vives were prescribed. In England they were required to be read at Eton College in 1561, at Westminster School about 1621, at Shrewsbury School 1562-1568, at Rivington Grammar School 1564, and Hertford Grammar School 1614. These ascertained and official instances are probably typical of very many others, both in England and abroad, of which the traces are lost.

### THE GREEK WORDS IN VIVES' DIALOGUES

One of the criticisms frequently urged against Vives is that he used Latinised Graecisms very frequently. It is not improbable that this very fact helped to secure the success of the book, for though there was by 1538 considerable enthusiasm in the aspiration of learning Greek, there was little knowledge of that language as yet even amongst the learned. To know even a small vocabulary of Greek words was a distinction, and to have such knowledge whilst learning to speak Latin was the basis for acquiring at least a smattering of Greek knowledge later on. Sir Thomas Elyot in his *Gouvernour* (1531) wishes the child " to learn Greek and Latin authors at the same time, or else to begin with Greek. If a child do begin therein at seven years of age, he may continually learn Greek authors three years, and in the meantime use the Latin as a familiar language." It was, no doubt, the desire of Vives, as of Sir Thomas Elyot, that children should learn as much as possible of Greek at the same time as Latin, and although the introduction of Greek words into the dialogues would not help the systematic study of Greek, it helped to create the atmosphere into which the study of Greek would find its place naturally enough in time.

The introduction of Greek words and phrases by Vives into his *School Dialogues* did not at any rate prevent the book from being in great demand, whilst the acknowledged difficulty of school teachers in translating the Greek terms brought about a series of expositions and commentaries on the *School Dialogues* that almost raised the book to the dignity of an ancient classical work. Issued first in 1538, in 1548 an edition was produced at Lyons with a commentary by Peter Motta and a Latin-Spanish index by Joannes Ramirus. In 1552, at Antwerp, Peter Motta's interpretation of Greek words, together with the old and somewhat obscure points in Vives, was supplemented by an alphabetical index of the more difficult words rendered into Spanish, French, and German. In 1553 Aegidius de Housteville published at Paris an edition, especially prepared for French boys, which gave the French for all difficult Latin words and included the commentary of Peter Motta.

## Euphrosynus Lapinius

In 1568 was published by Euphrosynus Lapinius at the Junta Press in Florence, an edition of Vives' *School Dialogues*. This also included the commentary of Peter Motta and, in addition, an index of certain words in Vives' *Dialogues*, with a translation of them into Etruscan.[1]

Vives' *School Dialogues*, we have seen, had a circulation, with vernacular vocabulary, in Spain, France, Germany, Italy (there does not seem to have been any edition with an English vocabulary). The inclusion of the Greek words, it is not unreasonable to suppose, met a need amongst learned schoolmasters, and since sufficient translations of the hard words, both Greek and Latin, were forthcoming, the book was made available even in those cases where schoolmasters had not sufficient knowledge to translate all the passages in which the pupils might stick.

## Style

Erasmus in his *Ciceronianus* thus describes the style of Vives: " I find lacking in Vives neither innate power, nor erudition, nor power of memory. He is well provided with luxuriance of expression even when, in the beginning of a

[1] This edition is not mentioned by Bömer.

work, he is a little hard; day by day his eloquence matures
more and more as he proceeds. . . . Daily he overcomes himself, and his genius is versatile enough for anything. Yet
sometimes he has not achieved some portion of the Ciceronian
virtues, especially in the direction of charm and mildness of
expression." (Quoted by Namèche, *Mémoire sur la vie et
les écrits de J. L. Vives.*)

## CHARACTERISTICS OF VIVES AS A WRITER OF DIALOGUES

Vives' characteristics have been well described by Bömer,
who says: " In the dialogues of Vives we constantly have
the pleasure of listening to conversations rich in thought,
made spicy at the right moments with pointed wit, so that
we are obliged to make an effort to understand the separate
words." It may be added that Vives is always desirous to
help forward the cause of learning, yet, on occasion, he can
detach himself from his learning and become a boy among
boys. He has a strong sense of humour. He can tell a joke
against himself, as for instance about his gout,[1] or again
about his singing.[2]

## VIVES AS A PRECURSOR OF THE DRAMA

It might, with some ground, be urged that Vives and
other writers of school dialogues are the precursors of the
drama. For not only are there touches of wit and humour
in the conversations, but there is a considerable amount of
characterisation in the interlocutors. The right person says
and does the right thing, and situations are sometimes hit
off exquisitely with an epithet. It is clear that a training in
following the school dialogues in the generation preceding the

[1] *See* p. xxvi.          [2] *See* p. 196-7.

Elizabethan dramatists may have had a distinctly prepara-
tive place in rendering the dialogue of the drama more
familiar and attractive as a literary method. For a preparation in the power of audiences following the dialogues
of the Elizabethan drama may be regarded as requiring an
explanation, when we remember that the interest in and
concentration on the dialogue was more urgent than now,
owing to the absence of scenery and the other visual effects
to which we are accustomed. The element in the drama
which is conspicuous by its absence in the school dialogues
is the plot. Yet in the school dialogue there is a definite
method of construction observed. In the old methods of
Latin composition, wherever there is a thesis, the writer
must have regard to the sequence of the introduction, the
narration, the confirmation, confutation, and the conclusion.

With regard to the school training towards the appreciation of the drama in the Tudor age, it must be remembered
that the school-play was a recognised institution, especially
the acting of the old plays of Terence, Plautus, and eventually of Greek tragedies. The school dialogue, it should be
noted, was one of the earliest of school text-books, and its
object, as already stated, was to train the child in readiness
of expression in *the speaking* of Latin. The study of rhetoric
followed, and this included not only the study of apt figures
of speech in Latin conversation, but also the accompaniment
of right gestures of the face, hands, and body. Hence it
will be seen that the grammar schools of the early part of
the sixteenth century paved the way for an intelligent
appreciation of the Elizabethan drama. For the drama not
only requires writers; to some extent an intelligent response
is necessary in the spectators, at any rate when the plays
involve the intellectual elements characteristic of the later
part of the sixteenth-century drama in England.

## Some Educational Aspects of Vives' Dialogues

It is remarkable that an elementary text-book for teaching
boys to speak Latin should raise so many fundamental
questions in the theory of education.    But any presentation
of the *Dialogues* of Vives would seem to be incomplete which
left unconsidered such points as Vives' *idea of the school, of the
school-games, of nature study, of the use of the vernacular in the
school*, and Vives' *view of the relation of religion and education*.

## Vives' Idea of the School

We learn from another book of Vives, the *De Tradendis
Disciplinis* (1531), that the " true academy," as he calls
his ideal school, is " the association together and fellow
sympathy of men equally good and learned, who have
come together themselves for the sake of learning, and to
render the same blessing to others." Vives suggests that
to such a " school " not only should boys go, but also men.
He suggests that " even old men, driven hither and thither
in a great tempest of ignorance and vice, should betake
themselves to the academy as it were to a haven.   In short,
let all be attracted by a certain majesty and authority."
Further, Vives informs us that in this academy it would
certainly be best to place boys there from their infancy,
" where they may from the first imbibe the best morals, and
evil behaviour will be to them new and detestable." We
thus see that " the academy " combines our so-called
elementary, secondary, and university education.   The idea
of the continuity of education is thus firmly conceived by
Vives, and, in addition, the action and reaction of different
ages of the individual scholars of the academy on one
another.   Nowadays, we realise that the association together

of those with the same limitations, *e.g.*, orphans, the blind, the deaf, may be a necessary evil, but that every progressive educational effort should be made to help all those who suffer from such limitations to become capable of taking their places amongst the normal pupils.   But Vives goes much further; with him, it is a defect in education to isolate the young from the old, the old from the young.   If all be bent on learning and scholarship, the differences of age disappear as clearly as the differences of rank and wealth.

It is necessary to bear in mind this conception of the academy in reading the school dialogues, for we have in them little children learning their alphabet [1] and the elements of reading [2] and writing,[3] and we have also the youths (at our undergraduate stage) going on their academic journey on horseback from Paris to Boulogne.   This reminds us of Milton's sallying forth of students " at the vernal seasons of the year, when the air is calm and pleasant, and it were an injury and sullenness against nature not to go out and see her riches and partake in her rejoicing with heaven and earth."

And we have the student of mature age, in his dressing-gown, at midnight, pursuing his classical meditations.   Thus infancy, youth, manhood, all stages, come into the conception of education.   Education is a continuous process lasting throughout life, and for Vives the educational institution of " schools " should embody and make facilities for the achievment of that idea.   In passing, it should be remarked that John Milton, in his *Tractate of Education* (1644), and John Dury (1650), in his *Reformed School*, advocate what we may call the Vives-Academy view of school! [4]   It must occur

---

[1] p. 21.                [2] p. 18.                [3] p. 65.
[4] In the eighteenth century, the Nonconformist academies, which are of the first significance as educational institutions, probably, in many cases, already associated the stages of elementary, secondary, and university education in one institution.

to every reader of Vives' *De Tradendis Disciplinis* as highly
probable that Milton's hurriedly dashed-off and eloquent
tractate was written after a fairly recent perusal of Vives'
book.

## GAMES

The treatises on education in Tudor times have scarcely
been surpassed by any later works in their treatment of
physical education and advocacy of games. Particularly is
this so in England, for in that period were published Sir
Thomas Elyot's *Gouvernour* (1531), Roger Ascham's *Toxophilus* (1545), and Richard Mulcaster's *Positions* (1581).
But outstanding in their importance as these works were,
Vives in his *School Dialogues* makes an interesting supple-
mentary contribution.

Vives shows the value of " play " as an underlying spirit
of school work, for the school is a form of " ludus " or
play.[1] The little child, Corneliola, learns the alphabet
" playing," as indeed children had done at any rate from
the days of Quintilian. Indeed, one of the most charming
pictures of children provided by Vives is in Dialogue VI.,
which describes the mother, the boys Tulliolus, Lentulus,
Scipio, and the little girl Corneliola, on the return from school
of the boys, as they engage in children's play and discussion
of it. The games named in that dialogue are the games of
" nuts," " odd and even," dice-play, draughts, and playing
cards. Vives passes over the question of the moral obliquity
of dice-playing and card-playing, though much was said in
the Tudor period with regard to them.[2]

---

[1] The grammar school was called in Latin *Ludus literarius*.

[2] *E.g.*, John Northbrooke: *Treatise wherein Dicing, etc., . . . are reproved . . . Dialogue-wise*, 1579 (Reprinted by the Shakespeare
Society); Gilbert Walker: *A Manifest Detection of the most Vyle and*

Vives represents the school-boys playing dice and cards for counters, and in the case of the cards for money. But substantially he gives the picture of the play without combining a sermon. In passing, perhaps it is permissible to call attention to the pun in Dialogue XXI., where the Latin word *charta* is taken up ambiguously in the meaning of " map " as well as of " card." The discovery of America in 1492 was comparatively recent in 1539, and much interest was felt in geographical questions. It is a great mistake to suppose that the classical scholars like Vives were so wrapt up in meditations on antiquity that they did not realise the significance of contemporary events, and that educationalists were not eager to turn current incidents to use in the class-room.[1] An interesting example of the fascination of Vives in geographical discoveries is to be found in the dedication of the *De Tradendis Disciplinis* to the renowned King John III., King of Portugal, in which he relates the splendid deeds of the Portuguese in travel and discovery, which bring glory to descendants and the obligation to live up to their standard of achievement. In Dialogue XII., in the description of the entrance-hall of a house, a map is referred to in which " you have the world newly discovered by the Spanish navigations." [2]

But educationally more important than any description of the games of the period described by Vives is the state-

*Detestable Use of Dice-play*, 1552 (Reprinted by the Percy Society); and by educational writers, *e.g.*, Roger Ascham: *Toxophilus* (1545), and Laurence Humphrey: *The Nobles* (1560). William Horman, headmaster of Eton College School, in his *Vulgaria* (in 1519) holds the opinion: " It is a shame that young gentlemen should lose time at the dice and tables, cards and hazard."

[1] As to charts, *e.g.*, Sir Thomas Elyot, in the *Gouvernour* (1531), says: " I cannot tell what more pleasure should happen to a gentle wit than to behold in his own house (*i.e.*, in pictures and maps) everything that within all the world is contained."

[2] *See* p. 95.

ment made by him of the laws which should regulate all play. The account is given in Dialogue XXII. Vives describes his native city of Valencia by sending three characters, Borgia, Scintilla, Cabanillius, on a promenade through the streets. They come to a public tennis-court, where the game of tennis is described. They proceed to the Town Court of Justice, whereupon one of the characters, Scintilla, is requested to state the laws of play which he has previously mentioned a teacher, by name Anneus, had written on a tablet which he had hung in his bed-chamber.

The six laws of play according to Anneus are:—

1. *Quando Ludendum ?* The Time of Playing. — This should be when the mind or body has become wearied. Games are to refresh the mind and body, not for frivolity.

2. *Cum Quibus Ludendum ?* Our Companions in Play.— These should be those who bring to the game no other purpose than your own, viz., that of thorough rest from labour and freedom from mental strain.

3. *Quo Ludo ?* The Sort of Game.—It must be known well by all the players. It must serve for both bodily and mental recreation. It must not be merely a game of hazard.

4. *Qua Sponsione ?* As to Stakes.—Small stakes are justifiable if they increase interest in exercise without producing excitement or anxiety of mind. Big stakes do not make a game; they introduce the rack.

5. *Quemadmodum ?* The Manner of Play.—Win and lose with absolute equanimity. No game should serve to rouse anger. No oaths, swearing, deceit, sordidness.

6. *Quamdiu Ludendum ?* Length of Play.—Until one is refreshed and the hour of serious business calls.

## Nature Study

It has already been mentioned that Vives supplies a dialogue describing an academic journey.[1] Two of the characters thus discourse:—

*Misippus*. Look how softly the river flows by!   What a delightful murmur there is of the full crystal water amongst the golden rocks!   Do you hear the nightingale and the goldfinch?   Of a truth, the country round Paris is most delightful!

*Philippus*. How placidly the Seine flows in its current. . . .   Oh, how the meadow is clothed with a magic art.

*Missippus*. And by what a marvellous Artist!

*Philippus*. What a sweet scent is exhaled. . . .   Please sing some verses as you are wont to do.

Then Vives introduces some lines by Angelus Politian praising the joy of peaceful, silent days which pass by without the agitation of ambition and the allurement of luxury, with blamelessness, though we work as with the labour of the poor man.   Again[2]:—

*Bambalio*. Listen, there is the nightingale!

*Graculus*. Where is she?

*Bambalio*. Don't you see her there, sitting on that branch?   Listen how ardently she sings, nor does she leave off.

*Nugo*. (As Martial says) *Flet philomela nefas*. (The nightingale bemoans any injustice.)

*Graculus*. What a wonder she carols so sweetly when she is away from Attica where the very waves of the sea dash upon the shore, not without their rhythm.

Then Nugo tells the story of the nightingale and cuckoo.[3] One more instance.   Several boys are out for a morning walk:—

*Malvenda*. Don't let us take our walk as if in a rush, but slowly and gently. . . .

---

[1] Dialogue IX.                              [2] Dialogue VIII.

[3] Which J. T. Freigius duly notes is taken from Ovid: *Metamorphoses*, liber vi., and Vergil: *Eclogues*, vi.

*Joannius* [*after contemplating the view*]. There is no sense which has not
a lordly enjoyment! First, the eyes! what varied colours,
what clothing of the earth and trees, what tapestry! What
paintings are comparable with this view? . . . Not without
truth has the Spanish poet, Juan de Mena, called May the
pianter of the earth. Then the ear. How delightful to hear
the singing of birds, and especially the nightingale. Listen to
her (as she sings in the thicket) from whom, as Pliny says,
issues the modulated sound of the completed science of
music. . . . In very fact, you have, as it were, the whole
study and school of music in the nightingale. Her little ones
ponder and listen to the notes which they imitate. The tiny
disciple listens with keen intentness (would that our teachers
received like attention!) and gives back the sound. . . .
Add to this there is a sweet scent breathing in from every
side, from the meadows, from the crops, from the trees, even
from the fallow-land and neglected fields.

## WINE-DRINKING AND WATER-DRINKING

There can be little doubt even from the descriptions of
feasts in the *School Dialogues* of Vives, as well as of Mosel-
lanus and Erasmus, that drunkenness was not uncommon
even amongst teachers in the Tudor period.[1] Vives distinguished himself by boldly advocating the claims of
water against those of wines and beer. In Dialogue XI.,
"Getting dressed and a Morning Constitutional," we read
[speaking of the food for breakfast, after the walk]:—

*Malvenda*. Shall we have wine to drink?
*Bellinus*. By no means,—but beer, and that of the weakest, of yellow
Lyons, *or else pure and liquid water* drawn from the Latin or
Greek well.
*Malvenda*. Which do you call the Latin well and the Greek well?
*Bellinus*. Vives is accustomed to call the well close to the gate the
Greek well; that one further off he calls the Latin well. He
will give you his reasons for the names when you meet him.

J. T. Freigius, who is always ready to supply what Vives
omits, gives in his commentary the reasons for Vives. The
Greek well is the well close to the gate, because the Greek

---

[1] Vives gives an example in Pandulphus (Dialogue IX.).

language is closer to the sources of language; the " Latin "
well, for similar reasons, is further off from the gate.

In Dialogue XVII., called " The Banquet," we read:—

*Scopas.* Don't give one too much water (*i.e.* in his wine).   Don't you
       know the old proverb, " You spoil wine, when you pour
       water into it "?
*Democritus.* Yes, then you spoil both the water and the wine.
*Polaemon.* I would rather spoil them both than be spoiled by one of
       them.

But it is in Dialogue XVII., on " Drunkenness," that
Vives specially launches his thunderbolts against excessive
drinking.   With the institution of lessons on temperance
in schools under some Local Education Authorities in
England, we have a return to the methods of Vives.   For in
the school dialogue referred to we have the matter put very
strongly, and probably Vives' statements would not prove
unacceptable to modern teachers of this recently re-intro-
duced subject.   After describing the moral effects of drunkenness, one of the characters says: " Who would not prefer
to be shut up at home with a dog or a cat than with a
drunkard?   For those animals have more intellect in them
than the drunkard."   Another character remarks: "When
you drink, you treat wine as you like.   When you have
drunk, it will treat you as it likes."

## The Vernacular

It is surprising to find that though Vives, in 1538, produced his *School Dialogues* for the purpose of teaching
children to *speak* Latin, and though he regarded early and
thorough acquaintance with Latin, both for purposes of
speaking and writing, as the very mark and seal of a well-
educated man, there was no learned man of his age who
went so far in advocacy of the importance of the teaching in

the vernacular of the pupil at a still younger age. As this constitutes one of the grounds upon which the pre-eminence of Vives as an educationalist would be rested, as for instance in comparison with Erasmus, it may not be altogether irrelevant to quote here the translation of a passage from the *De Tradendis Disciplinis* explaining Vives' views on this subject.

" The scholars should first speak in their homes their mother tongue, which is born with them, and the teacher should correct their mistakes. Then they should, little by little, learn Latin. Next let them intermingle with the vernacular what they have heard in Latin from their teacher, or what they themselves have learned. Thus, at first, their language should be a mixture of the mother-tongue and Latin. But outside the school they should speak the mother-tongue so that they should not become accustomed to a hotch-potch of languages. . . . Gradually the development advances and the scholars become Latinists in the narrower sense. Now must they seek to express their thoughts in Latin, for nothing serves so much to the learning of a language as continuous practice in it. He who is ashamed to speak a language has no talent for it. He who refuses to speak Latin after he has been learning it for a year must be punished according to his age and circumstances." [1]

So much for the pupil's knowledge of the vernacular. Still more emphatically Vives speaks with regard to the necessity of a thorough knowledge of the vernacular by the *teacher*.

" Let the teacher know the mother-tongue of his boys, so that by this means, with the more ease and readiness, he may teach the learned languages. For unless he makes use of the right and proper expressions in the mother-tongue, he will certainly mislead the boys, and the error thus imbibed will accompany them persistently as they grow up and

[1] *De Tradendis Disciplinis*, book iii. chap. 3.

become men.  How can boys understand anything sufficiently well in their own language unless the words are said
with the utmost clearness.  Let the teacher preserve in his
memory all the old forms of vernacular words, and let him
develop the knowledge not only of modern forms, but also
of the old words and those which have gone out of use, and
let him be as it were the guardian of the treasury of his
language." [1]

## THE EDUCATIONAL IDEAL OF VIVES

It has been usual to enter to the credit of the Protestantism
of John Sturm and Maturinus Corderius the educational
ideal of *pietas literata*.  No doubt the seventeenth-century
Huguenots of France and the Puritans of England were distinguished by this double educational aim of piety and
culture.  But it was characteristic also of the earlier Catholic
world of Erasmus and of Vives.  Rising above the ordinary
level of the scholars of the Italian Renascence, Erasmus and
Vives had higher sympathy and delight in children.  Erasmus
dedicated his *Colloquia* or Dialogues (in 1524) to the little
child John Erasmius Froben, the son of the renowned
publisher Froben of Basle.  "You have arrived," he says,
"at an age than which none happier occurs in the course of
life for imbibing the seeds of literature and of piety. . . .
The Lord Jesus keep the present season of your life pure
from all pollutions, and ever lead you on to better things."

So, too, in 1538, Juan Luis Vives dedicated his *School Dialogues* to a child, the eleven-years-old boy—Prince Philip.

Both Erasmus and Vives believed in early training in
religious instruction.  Vives writes as follows on religious
education: "Who is there who has considered the power
and loftiness of the mind, its understanding of the most

[1] *De Tradendis Disciplinis*, book iii. chap. 3.

remarkable things, and through understanding love of them, and from love the desire to unite himself with them, who does not perceive clearly that man was formed, not for food, clothing, and habitation, not for difficult, secret, and vexatious knowledge, but to develop the desire to know God more truly, to participate in His Divine Nature and His Eternity? . . . Since piety is the only way of perfecting man, and accomplishing the end for which he was formed, therefore piety is of all things the one thing necessary. Without the others man can be perfected and complete; without this, he cannot but be most miserable."[1]

In one passage Vives remarks that the strength of religion is developed by its exercise rather than by any theoretical knowledge. For this reason, when meals are described in the *School Dialogues*, we find some form of grace, before and after the meal, duly said. The tone of the *Dialogues* is reverential. A. J. Namèche says[2] that in the *Dialogues* "Vives brings a sense of decency, respect for morals, the fear so laudable of doing any violence to the innocence of young people. We know well enough that Erasmus is far from being irreproachable in this respect, and that his language is free sometimes even to the extent of cynicism." Without wishing to follow Namèche in the comparison of the moral aspects of Erasmus and Vives in their dialogues, a claim may be made for both that they were eager advocates in the joining of piety with culture, and that both Erasmus and Vives, each in his own way, did valiant work in endeavouring to raise the standard of manners and morals as well as to promote piety in young and old.

There can, however, be no doubt that Vives deserved the high reputation which he received of reverence for the morals

---

[1] *De Tradendis Disciplinis*, book i. chap. 2.
[2] *Mémoire sur la vie et les écrits de J. L. Vives*, p. 87.

of youth. Peter Motta is full of enthusiasm for Vives in this respect. In the Preface to his *Commentary on Vives' School Dialogues*, Motta says: " By reading other books such as those of Terence and Plautus, you can undoubtedly get extracts which show the fruit of eloquence. But who can avoid seeing that in them you will find incitements to vices, and stumbling blocks to morals? Now, in our author Vives, you will find little flowers of Latin elegance which he has brought together from various most renowned authors, whilst there is nothing in his work which does not seem to suggest even the Christ, or at least the highest morality and sound education." This may be regarded as the exaggerated language of an admirer, but the reverential tone of Vives is clear enough, reminding one of Vittorino da Feltre, of whom it was said that he went to his teacher's desk each day as if to an altar.

### Vives' Last Dialogue: The Precepts of Education

Vives lays down twenty-four Precepts of Education. Some critics have thought such precepts out of place in a book written for boys. But Vives has done all he could to interest boys on their own level. He has always retained the boy in himself, and has spoken from the fulness of his heart, as a boy, in the dialogues. And as he parts company with boys in these dialogues, he wishes, as all true, older human beings must wish, for once at least to give of his best to the young. He will give back to the boys who have followed him through the *Dialogues* (as a teacher who is a " good sort ") a full reward for their trouble. He will pay them the compliment of treating them seriously.

This seems a right instinct. It is not priggish (as some seem to think) to give of a man's best to a boy or to boys at the right moment. When once a boy is sure there is " the boy " in any man he knows, there is no *camaraderie* he delights in such as that which allows him to see a little of the man,— to jump, so to say, on the man's mental shoulders to catch a better glimpse of the far distance.

When John Thomas Freigius—grown up into the classical scholar—looks back, in his Preface to his edition of Vives' *School Dialogues*, he says: " As a boy, I so loved Luis Vives that not even now do I feel my old love for him has faded away from my mind." Perhaps the last dialogue, with its twenty-four precepts, did not cause the love of Freigius for Vives, but the love being there, it continued in spite of having to read the precepts. Anyway, Vives, who had turned aside from the weighty problems of learning and literature, where he belonged to the great triumvirate of writers of his day—enthroned by contemporary judges by the side of the great Erasmus and the great Budaeus—stated the precepts which, in his view, should guide, not only his book of dialogues and the schools, but all stages of culture. Boys brought up on these precepts, and retaining them as principles of education in their later life, might perhaps have cheered the heart of Vives by showing that he had abstained from his higher studies to some purpose when he wrote his *School Dialogues*.

At any rate, for the modern reader, there is the satisfaction of knowing, when he reads the *School Dialogues* of Vives, that he is reading a work which won the approval of children. With all our modern advance, of which of the writers of our text-books to-day would present-day children say as much as was said of this sixteenth-century scholar, who merely wrote a text-book to help boys of the Tudor Age to *speak Latin !*—" As a boy I so loved Luis Vives that not even now do I feel my old love for him has faded away from my mind."

## NOTE

The short summaries or headings to each dialogue in the text are translations from the edition of Vives' *Dialogues* by John Thomas Freigius, published at Nürnberg, 1582. After each dialogue Freigius provides a commentary, by far the most complete of any commentator on Vives' book, giving illustrative quotations and notes on obscure points, and giving references to the ancient sources from which technical expressions were taken by Vives. The headings of the sub-sections of each dialogue as given in the present translation are taken from Freigius. They are not a part of the original text of Vives.

The above is the most scholarly and thorough edition of the *Dialogues*, but it may be noted that Dr. Bömer [1] has distinguished over *one hundred* editions of the book, showing its popularity not only in the sixteenth century but its continued interest in still later generations of the study of Latin speech.

---

[1] *Die lateinischen Schülergespräche der Humanisten*, pp. 163-7.

# TUDOR SCHOOL-BOY LIFE

## I

### SURRECTIO MATUTINA—*Getting up in the Morning*

BEATRIX PUELLA, EMANUEL, EUSEBIUS

Dialogue (Latin—*colloquium, collocutio, sermo*) is so called from διαλέγεως, in which sort of composition Plato was the first to delight. In this first dialogue or discourse (*sermone*) there are laid down five duties, which should be performed care-/ fully in the morning by youths and boys, viz. to rise betimes (because early morning is the friend to studies), to dress, to comb the hair, to wash, to pray.

*Beat.* May Jesus Christ awake you from the sleep of all vice. O you boys, are you ever going to wake up to-day?

*Euseb.* I don't know what has fallen on my eyes. I seem to have them full of sand.

### I. *Getting Up*

*Beat.* That is always your morning song—quite an old one. I shall open both the wooden and the glass windows, so that the morning shall strike brightly on your eyes from both. Get up! Get up!

*Euseb.* Is it already morning?

## II. *Dressing*

*Beat.* It is nearer mid-day than the dawn. Emanuel, do you want another shirt?

*Eman.* I don't now need anything. This is clean enough. I will take another to-morrow. Please give me my stomacher.

*Beat.* Which? The single thickness or the double thickness?

*Eman.* Which you like. I don't mind. Give me the single thickness so that I may be less heavy for playing ball (*pila*) to-day.

*Beat.* This is always your custom. You think of your play before your school-work.

*Eman.* What do you say, you stupid! When school itself is called play (*ludus*).

*Beat.* I don't understand your playing with grammar and logic (*grammaticationes et sophismata*).

*Eman.* Give me the leathern shoe-straps.

*Beat.* They are torn to pieces. Take the silken ones as your schoolmaster has ordered. What now? Will you have the breeches and long stockings as it is summer?

*Eman.* No, indeed. Give me only the long stockings. Please, fasten them for me.

*Beat.* What! Have you arms of hay or of butter?

*Eman.* No, indeed. They are sewn together with threads. Alas! what straps (*i.e.* points) have you given me, without supports and all torn!

*Beat.* Don't you remember that yesterday at dice-playing you lost the others altogether?

*Eman.* How do you know?

*Beat.* I observed you through a chink in the door as you were playing with Guzmanulus.

*Eman.* Oh! I beg that you won't tell the teacher.

*Beat.* No, but I will tell him if ever you call me " ugly " again, as you are accustomed to do.

*Eman.* What if I call you greedy?

*Beat.* Call me what you will, but not ugly.

*Eman.* Give me my shoes.

*Beat.* Which? Those with the long straps (*i.e.* sandals)?

*Eman.* Those covered against the mud.

*Beat.* Against the dry mud, which they call dust. But thou doest well, for on the open road the strap gets broken and the buckle lost.

*Eman.* Put them on, I beg.

*Beat.* Do it yourself.

*Eman.* I cannot bend myself.

*Beat.* You could easily bend, but your laziness makes it difficult, or have you swallowed a sword as the mountebank did four days ago? Are you now so delicate? What will happen to you as you grow up?

*Eman.* Tie a double knot—for it is more elegant.

*Beat.* Certainly not, for then the knot would be loosened at that point and the shoe would fall from your foot. It is better either to have a double drawing tight or one knot and one loop. Take your tunic with long sleeves and your woven girdle.

*Eman.* No, certainly not that, but the leathern hunting girdle.

*Beat.* Your mother forbids that; do you wish to have everything according to your own caprice? And yesterday you broke the pin of the clasp!

*Eman.* I could not otherwise unbuckle it. Then give me that red one made of linen cloth.

### III. *Using the Comb*

*Beat.* Take it, put your French girdle on. Comb your head first with the thinner, then with the thicker teeth, place your cap on your head, so as not to throw it to the back of your head, as is your custom, or on to your forehead down to your eyes.

*Eman.* Let us at last go out.

*Beat.* What, without having washed your hands and face!

*Eman.* With your worrying curiosity you would have already plagued a bull to death, let alone a man. You think you are clothing not a boy, but a bride.

### IV. *Washing*

*Beat.* Eusebius, bring a wash-basin and a pitcher. Raise it to a fair height; let the water drop out rather than pour it from the stopple. Wash thoroughly that dirt from the joints of the fingers. Cleanse the mouth and use water for gargling. Rub the eyelids and eyebrows, then the glands of the neck under the ears vigorously. Then take a cloth and dry yourself. Immortal God! that it should be necessary to admonish you as to all these things, one by one, and that you should do nothing of your own thought.

*Eman.* Ah! you are too much of a boss and too rude!

### V. *Prayer*

*Beat.* And you are too shrewd and pretty a boy. Come, give me a kiss. Kneel down before this image of our Saviour and say the Lord's Prayer and the other prayers, as you are accustomed, before you step out of your bedroom. Take care, my Emanuel, that you think of nothing else while you are praying. Stay a moment, hang this little handkerchief on your girdle, so that you can blow and clean your nose.

*Eman.* Am I now sufficiently prepared, in your opinion?

*Beat.* You are.

*Eman.* Then not in my opinion since at last I am in yours. I will dare make a wager that I have taken up a whole hour in dressing.

*Beat.* Well, what even if you had taken two? Where would you have gone if you hadn't? What were you going to do? I suppose to dig or to plough?

*Eman.* As if there were a lack of something to do.

*Beat.* Oh, the great man! so keenly occupied in doing nothing.

*Eman.* Won't you go away, you girl sophist? Go, or I'll shy this shoe at you or tear the veil off your head.

## II

### PRIMA SALUTATIO—*Morning Greetings*

Puer, Mater, Pater—Boy, Mother, Father

In this dialogue there are three parts: the first contains the mutual salutations expressed in the morning when the little charms of early childhood are skilfully displayed. The second part contains the sport of a boy with a dog. The third gives a conversation with this boy concerning the school, the opportunity for which arises from the incident with the little dog.

### I. *Morning Salutation*

*Boy.* Hail, my father! hail, my mother dear (*salve mea matercula*)! I wish that this may be a happy day for you, my little brothers (*germanuli*). May Christ be propitious to you, my little sisters!

*Father.* My son, may God guard you and lead you to great goodness (*ingentes virtutes*).

*Mother.* May Christ preserve you, my light. What are you doing, my darling? How are you? How did you rest last night?

*Boy.* I am very well and slept peacefully.

*Mother.* Thanks be to Christ! May He grant that this may be constantly so!

*Boy.* In the middle of the night I was roused up with a pain in the head.

*Mother.* It grieves me sorely to hear that (*me per-*
6

*ditam et miserrimam*)! What do you say? In
what part of the head?

*Boy.* In the forehead.

*Mother.* For how long?

*Boy.* Scarcely the eighth of an hour. Afterwards I fell
asleep again, nor did I feel anything further
of it.

*Mother.* Now I breathe again; for you took away my
breath.

## II. *Playing with the Dog*

*Boy.* All good to you! Little Isabel, prepare my breakfast. Ruscio, Ruscio, come here, jolly little
dog! See how he fawns with his tail and
how he raises himself on his hind legs. What
are you doing? How are you? Hullo, you,
bring a bit or two of bread which we may give
him, then you will see some clever sport.
Won't you eat? Haven't you had anything
to-day? Clearly there is more intelligence in
that dog than in that crass mule-driver.

## III. *The Father's Little Talk with his Boy*

*Father.* My Tulliolus, I should like to have a talk with
you soon.

*Boy.* Why, my father? For nothing more delightful
could happen to me than to listen to you.

*Father.* Is thy Ruscio here an animal or a man?

*Boy.* An animal, as I think.

*Father.* What have you in you, why you should be a
man and not he? You eat, drink, sleep,

walk, run, play.  So he does all these things also.

*Boy.* But I am a man.

*Father.* How do you know this?  What have you now, more than a dog?  But there is this difference that he cannot become a man.  You can, if you will.

*Boy.* I beg of you, my father, bring this about as soon as possible.

*Father.* It will be done if you go where animals go, to come back men.

*Boy.* I will go, father, with all the pleasure in the world!  But where is it?

*Father.* In the school.

*Boy.* There is no delay in me for such a great matter.

*Father.* Nor in me.  Isabel, dear, do you hear, give him his breakfast in this little satchel.

*Isabel.* What shall it be?

*Father.* A piece of bread and butter, and dry figs, or pressed, not dried, grapes, as an additional dish —for fresh grapes besmear the fingers of boys and they spoil their clothes—unless he should prefer a few cherries, or golden and long plums. Hang the satchel on his little arm, so that it shall not fall off.

# III

## DEDUCTIO AD LUDUM—*Escorting to School*

Pater, Puer, Propinquus, Philoponus Ludimagister—
Father, Boy, Relative, Philoponus the Schoolmaster

*Philoponus.*—This name, so worthy of a teacher, has been
rightly and wisely bestowed by the author. For the true
teacher ought to be φιλόπονος, that is, φίλος τοῦ πονοῦ, a lover
of labour, and by his diligence and assiduity to give satisfaction
to his pupils. But Philoponus is, moreover, the proper name of
the Greek interpreter of Aristotle.

### Consultation as to a Teacher

*Father.* Make the holy sign of the cross.

*Son.* Lead us ignorant ones, O most wise Jesus Christ,
Thou most powerful, lead us most weak!

*Father.* Inform me, I beg, thou who art most versed in
the study of letters, who in this school is the
best teacher of boys?

*Prop.* The most learned is a certain Varro; but the most
industrious and the most upright is Philoponus, whose erudition, moreover, is not to be
despised. Varro has the best frequented
school, and in his house he has a numerous
flock of boarders. Philoponus does not seem
to delight in numbers, but is content with
fewer boys.

*Father.* I should prefer him. That must be he walking

9

into the hall of the school. Son, this is, as it were, the laboratory for the formation of men, and he is the artist-educator. Christ be with you, master! Uncover your head, my boy, and bow your right knee, as you have been taught. Now, stand up!

*Philoponus.* May your coming be a blessing to us all! What may be your business?

*Father.* I bring you this boy of mine for you to make of him a man from the beast.

*Philoponus.* This shall be my earnest endeavour. He shall become a man from a beast, a fruitful and good creature out of a useless one. Of that have no doubt.

*Father.* What is the charge for your instruction?

*Philoponus.* If the boy makes good progress, it will be little; if not, a good deal.

*Father.* That is acutely and wisely said, as is all you say. We share the responsibility then; you, to instruct zealously, I to recompense your labour richly.

# IV

## EUNTES AD LUDUM LITERARIUM—*Going to School*

CIRRATUS, PRAETEXTATUS, TITIVILLITIUM, TERESULA (AN OLD
WOMAN, A WOMAN SELLER OF VEGETABLES)

The names of the interlocutors in this dialogue for the most
part signify something serious and ancient. *Cirrati pueri* were
those boys who wore their hair curled and crisped. Krausz Haar.
For the *cirrus* is an instrument devised for the curling of hair.

*Martial :*
> Nec matutini cirrata caterva magistri.

*Juvenal :* Flavam
> Caesariem et madido torquentem cornua cirro.

*Persius*, Satyr, i.:
> Ten' cirratarum centum dictata fuisse
> Pro nihilo pendas?

*Praetextatus puer* is another way of referring to a noble or
patrician, for his outer garment was bordered with purple, and
thus worn by boys up to fourteen years of age, or as others say,
up to sixteen, when such an one assumed the *toga virilis* in the
Capitol. *See* Macrob. lib. i. *Satur.* cap. 6. Budae, in prior.
annot. ad l. fin. De senator. Alexand. lib. 2, cap. 25. Baysius, de re vestiment. Sigonius, lib. 3, de judic. cap. 19. Pap-
irius, a certain Roman, was called *praetextatus* because in the
*praetextata* age he showed the height of prudence. *See* Macrob.

*Titivillitium* formerly was a word declaring nothing certain,
but just an exclamation, indicating extreme uncertainty. The
word was used by Plautus. *See* Proverb, Titivillitium.

*Oluscularia*, a woman selling vegetables. Λαχανοπῶλις.

*Cirr.* Does it seem to you to be time to go to school?
*Praet.* Certainly, it is time to go.

*Cirr.* I don't properly remember the way; I believe we have to go through this next street.

*Praet.* How often have you already been to the school?

*Cirr.* Three or four times.

*Praet.* When did you first go?

*Cirr.* As I think, three or four days ago.

*Praet.* Well, now; isn't that enough to enable you to know the way?

*Cirr.* No, not if it were a hundred times of going.

*Praet.* Why, if I were to go once, never afterwards should I miss the way. But you go, against your will, and as you go, you stop and play. You don't look at the way, nor at the houses, nor any signs which would show you afterwards which way you should turn, or which way you should follow. But I observe all these points diligently, because I go gladly.

*Cirr.* This boy lives quite close to the school. Here, you, Titivillitium, which is the way to your house?

*Tit.* What do you want? Do you come from your mother? My mother is not at home, nor even my sister. Both have gone out to St. Anne's.

*Cirr.* What then is to be done?

*Tit.* Yesterday was dedication festival (*encaenia*). To-day some woman who sells cheese has invited them to a meal at the house called "Thick Milk" (*lac coagulatum*).

*Cirr.* And why haven't you gone with them?

*Tit.* They have left me at home to keep house. They

have taken my little brother with them, but they have promised me that they would bring back something of what was left for me in a basket.

*Cirr.* But why art thou then not remaining at home?

*Tit.* I shall return immediately, only I will now play dice a little with the son of this cobbler. Will you also come with us?

*Cirr.* We will go, please.

*Praet.* Certainly I shall not do so.

*Cirr.* Why not?

*Praet.* We don't want to get a thrashing.

*Cirr.* Ah! I had not thought of that.

*Tit.* You won't get thrashed.

*Cirr.* How do you know that?

*Tit.* Because your master lost his rod (*ferula*) to-day.

*Cirr.* Eh! by what means did you get to know that?

*Tit.* To-day we heard him from our house shouting out —and it was for his ferula he was seeking.

*Cirr.* I beg of you, let us play for a short time.

*Praet.* Play you, if you will; but I shall go on to school at once.

*Cirr.* I beg of you, don't report me to the master. Say that I am kept by my father at home.

*Praet.* Do you wish me to tell a lie?

*Cirr.* Why not, for a friend's sake?

*Praet.* Because I have heard a preacher in a church declare that liars are the sons of the devil, but truth-tellers, sons of God.

*Cirr.* Of the devil, indeed! Get away! By the sign of the holy cross, may our God free us from our enemies!

*Praet.* Thou canst not be freed to play when thou oughtest to go and learn.

*Cirr.* Let us go. Farewell.

*Tit.* Oh, I say! these boys dare not stay and play a moment because otherwise they would get thrashed!

*Praet.* This boy is a waster and will become a bad man! See how has he slipped away from us without our having asked him which is the way to the school? Let us call him back.

*Cirr.* Let him go his evil ways. I don't wish him again to invite me to play. We will inquire from this old woman. Mother, do you know which is the way to the school of Philoponus?

*Old Woman.* I have lived near this school for six years, just opposite to it where my eldest son and two daughters were born. You cross this street (the *Villa Rasa* Street), then comes a narrow lane, then the *Dominus Veteranus* Street. Hence you turn to the right, then to the left, there you must inquire, for the school is not far from there.

*Cirr.* Ah! we cannot remember all that!

*Old Woman.* My little Teresa, lead these boys to the school of Philoponus, for the mother of this one here was she who gave us the thread for combing and spinning.

*Ter.* What in the name of evil have you to do with Philoponus? What sort of mar is this Philoponus? As if I knew him! Do you speak of the man who mends shoes near the Green Inn (*cauponam viridem*) or of the herald in the Giant Street, who keeps horses on hire?

*Old Woman.* This I know well, that you never know those things which are wanted, but those which have nothing to do with the matter in hand. Slowest of girls, Philoponus is that old schoolmaster, tall, short - sighted man, opposite the house where we used to live.

*Ter.* Ah! now it comes back to my mind.

*Old Woman.* In returning, go across the market and buy salad, radish, and cherries. Take with you the little basket.

*Cirr.* Lead us also over the vegetable market.

*Ter.* This way is shorter.

*Cirr.* We don't wish to go that way.

*Ter.* Why so?

*Cirr.* Because the dog in that street, belonging to the baker, bit me once. We would rather go with you to the market.

*Ter.* Returning I will make the journey through the market (for we are not far from it) and I will buy what I was told to buy, after I have left you at the school.

*Cirr.* We desire to see how much you give for the cherries.

*Ter.* We buy them at six farthings a pound; but what is that to you?

*Cirr.* Because my sister ordered me this morning to inquire. She particularly mentioned there is an old woman in the market who sells vegetables. If you buy of her, I know that she will sell you at a less price than they will elsewhere, and she will give us a few cherries or thyrsus of lettuce, for her daughter formerly served my mother and sister.

*Ter.* I hope that this roundabout way may not let you in for some lashes.

*Cirr.* Not at all. For we shall have plenty of time.

*Ter.* Let us go. I get so little chance of walks, wretched that I am, for my time is all taken up sitting at home.

*Praet.* What do you do? Do you merely sit idly at home?

*Ter.* Idly, indeed! Not at any rate that! I spin, I gather (wool) into a ball, wind, weave. Do you think our old woman would let me sit idle? She curses feast-days, on which there must be a stoppage of work.

*Praet.* Are not feast-days holy? How can she curse what is holy? Does she wish to curse what has been ordained as holy?

*Ter.* Do you think that I have learned geometry that I should be able to explain these things to you?

*Cirr.* What do you mean by geometry?

*Ter.* I don't know. We had a neighbour who was called Geometria. She was always either in church with priests, or the priests were with her at her house. And so she was, as they said, very wise.—But we have come into the vegetable market. Where is now your old woman?

*Cirr.* I was looking round about for her. But buy of her only on the condition that she gives us something as a present. Ah! great-aunt (*amita*). This girl will buy cherries of you, if you will give us some.

*Vegetable Woman.* We are given nothing; we have to buy everything.

*Cirr.* That dirt which you have on your hands and neck was not given to you, was it?

*Vegetable Woman.* Unless you take yourself off, you impudent boy, your cheeks will feel some of this dirt on them.

*Cirr.* How will my cheeks feel, when you have it on your hands?

*Vegetable Woman.* Give those cherries back, you young rogue.

*Cirr.* I am merely sampling, for I wish to buy.

*Vegetable Woman.* Then buy.

*Cirr.* Provided they have pleased me. How do you sell them?

*Vegetable Woman.* A sesterce a pound.

*Cirr.* Ah! they are bitter, you old poisoner! You are selling here cherries to people to choke them.

*Ter.* Let us go away to the school. For you will get me involved in difficulties with your subtleties, and you will detain me too long. Now, as I think, my old woman is raging at home, on account of my delay in returning. There is the door. Knock at it.

# V

## LECTIO—*Reading*

PRAECEPTOR, LUSIUS, AESCHINES, PUERI—Teacher,
Lusius, Aeschines, Boys

*Lusius*, so called from playing (*ludendo*).
*Aeschines*, proper name of the Greek orator, who shamelessly declaimed against Demosthenes.
*Cotta*, proper name of a Roman citizen, so called from his anger.
This dialogue contains a division of the letters into vowels and consonants.

*Praec.* Take the A B C tablet in your left hand, and
this pointer in the right hand, so that you can
point out the letters , one by one. Stand
upright; put your cap under your arm-pit.
Listen most attentively how I shall name these
letters. Look diligently how I move my
mouth. See that you return what I say immediately in the same manner, when I ask for
it again. Attention (*sis mecum*)! Now you
have heard it. Follow me now as I say it
before you, letter by letter. Do you clearly
understand?

*Lus.* It seems to me I do, fairly well.

### *Letters—Syllables—Vowel—Speech*

*Praec.* Every one of these signs is called a letter. Of
these, five are vowels, A, E, I, O, U. They

18

are in the Spanish *oveia*, which signifies *sheep*.
Remember that word! These with any letter
you like, or more than one, make up syllables.
Without a vowel there is no syllable and sometimes the vowel itself is a syllable. Therefore
all the other letters are called consonants,
because they don't constitute sounds by themselves unless a vowel is joined to them. They
have some imperfect, maimed (*mancum*) sound,
*e.g. b, c, d, g,* which without *e* cannot be
sounded. Out of syllables we get words, and
from words connected speech, which all beasts
lack. And you would not be different
from the beasts, if you could not converse
properly. Be watchful and perform your work
diligently. Go out with your fellow-pupils
and learn what I have set.

*Lus.* We are not playing to-day.

*Aesch.* No, for it is a work-day. What, do you think
you have come here to play? This is not the
place for playing, but for study.

*Lus.* Why, then, is a school called *ludus ?*

### True Leisure

*Aesch.* It is indeed called *ludus*, but it is *ludus literarius*,
because here we must play with letters as else-
where with the ball, hoop, and dice. And I
have heard that in Greek it is called *schola*, as
it were a place of leisure, because it is true
ease and quiet of mind, when we spend our
life in studies. But we will learn thoroughly
what the teacher has bidden us, quite in soft

murmur, so that we don't become a hindrance to one another.

*Lus.* My uncle, who studied letters some time in Bologna, has taught me that you better fix anything you wish in the memory if you pronounce it aloud. This is also confirmed by the authority of one called Pliny—I don't know who he was.

*Aesch.* If, then, any one should wish to learn his *formulae*, he should go off into the garden or into the churchyard. There he can shout aloud as if he would rouse the dead.

*Cotta.* You boys, do you call this learning thoroughly? I call it prattling and disputing! Up, now go all of you to the teacher, as he commanded.

# VI

## REDITUS DOMUM ET LUSUS PUERILIS—
### *The Return Home and Children's Play*

TULLIOLUS, CORNELIOLA, LENTULUS, SCIPIO

This dialogue contains an account of different kinds of boys' games; the names of the interlocutors are taken from appelations of the Romans. Concerning which, *see* Valer. Maximus and Sigonius.

*Corn.* Welcome home, Tulliolus, shall we have some games?

*Tull.* Not just now.

*Corn.* What is there to prevent us playing?

*Tull.* We must go over again what the master set, and commit it to memory, as he bade us.

*Corn.* What then?

*Tull.* You just look at this.

*Corn.* I say, what are those pictures? I believe they are pictures of ants. Mother mine, Tulliolus is bringing a lot of ants and gnats painted on a writing-tablet.

*Tull.* Be quiet, you silly thing, they are letters.

*Corn.* What do you call this first one?

*Tull.* A.

*Corn.* Why is this first one rather than the next called A?

*Mother.* Why art thou Corneliola and not Tulliolus?

*Corn.* Because I am so called.

*Mother.* And it is just the same way with those letters.
But go and play now, my boy.

*Tull.* I am putting my tablet and pencil (style) down
here.   If anybody disturbs them, he will be
beaten by mother.   Won't he, mammy? (*mea
matercula.*)

*Mother.* Yes, my boy.

*Tull.* Scipio, Lentulus!   Come and play.

*Sci.* What shall we play at?


I. *The Game of Nuts*

*Tull.* Let us play at nuts, at throwing them in holes.

*Lent.* I have only a few nuts and those squashed and
smelly.

*Sci.* Well then, we will play with the shells of nuts.

*Tull.* But what good would they be to me even if I
were to win twenty? There would be no
kernels in the nuts for me to eat.

*Sci.* Why, I don't eat when I am playing.   If I want to
eat, I go to the mater.   Nut-shells are good
for making little houses to put ants into.


II. *The Game of Odd and Even*

*Lent.* Let us play odd and even with little pins (lit.
small pins for a head-dress—*acicula*).

*Tull.* Let's have dice instead.

*Sci.* Fetch them, Lentulus.

*Lent.* Here are the dice.

### III. *The Game of Dice*

*Tull.* How grubby and dirty they are. They are not free from fluff. Nor are they polished. Cast!

*Sci.* For the first throw!

*Tull.* I am first. What are we playing?

*Sci.* We are playing for trousers buttons (*astrigmenta*— lit. points).

*Lent.* I don't want to lose mine, for if I did I should be beaten at home by my tutor.

*Tull.* What are you willing to lose then, if you are beaten?

*Lent.* Some good raps with the fingers on me.

*Mother.* What is that lying on the ground? You are spoiling all your clothes and boots on the dirtiest of the ground. Why don't you first sweep the floor and then sit down? Bring the broom here!

*Tull.* What have we decided on?

*Sci.* One needle for each point in the game.

*Tull.* Certainly it should be two.

*Lent.* I have no needles. If you like I will deposit cherry-stones instead of needles.

*Tull.* Get away. Let me and you play, Scipio.

*Sci.* I will risk it—to cast my needle on luck.

*Tull.* Give me the dice in my hand, so that I may cast first. Look, I have won the stake.

*Sci.* You haven't. For you were not playing then in serious.

*Tull.* Whoever *plays* seriously? It is as if you spoke of a white Moor.

*Sci.* You may cavil as much as you like. At any rate you are not going to have my nuts.

*Tull.* Come now, I will let you have the throw. Let us play now for the stake, and may you have good luck!

*Sci.* You are beaten.

*Tull.* Take it.

*Lent.* Let me have the dice.

*Tull.* Let's stake all on this throw.

*Lent.* I don't mind.

*A Servant.* To your meal, boys, Will you never make an end of your games?

*Tull.* Now just as we are getting started, she talks of stopping!

### IV. *The Game of Draughts*

*Corn.* I am sick of this game. Let us play with the two-coloured draughtsmen.

*Tull.* You paint for us squares on this surface with charcoal and with white lime.

*Sci.* I prefer to go and have my supper to playing any more, and I go with all my needles collared by your fraud.

*Tull.* Don't you remember that yesterday you plundered Cethegus. " There is no one who can always have luck in play."

### V. *Playing Cards*

*Corn.* Please get the playing cards which you will find on the left hand under the writing table.

*Sci.* Some other time. Now I haven't time. If I

delay any longer, I fear that my teacher will send me to bed, in his anger, without food. You get the cards ready for to-morrow evening, Corneliola.

*Corn.* If mother permits, it would be better to play now when we have the chance.

*Sci.* It is better to go to eat when we are called.

*Servant.* And don't you give me anything for looking on?

*Corn.* We would give you something if you had acted as umpire. You ought rather to give us something, as things are, for having had the enjoyment of our play.

*Servant.* You boys, then, when are you coming? The meal - time is half over; soon we shall take the meat away, and set the cheese and fruit on the table.

# VII

## REFECTIO SCHOLASTICA—*School Meals*

NEPOTULUS, PISO, MAGISTER, HYPODIDASCALUS

In this dialogue Vives treats of a banquet. The division into five parts:—

Jentaculum ⎫
Prandium ⎪
Merenda  ⎬ An enumeration
Coena  ⎪ of different kinds.
Comessatio ⎭

*See* Grap. lib. 2, cap. 3.

He describes convivial disputations.

*Nepotulus* is a diminutive from nepos, used for one who drinks.

*Piso* is a young nobleman.

*Hypodidascalus*, ὁ ὑπώ τὲ διδασκαλον, provisor, cantor.

In the beginning of this dialogue there are three αμφιβολίας or ambiguities. The first is in the adverb *lautè*, the signification of which is twofold, one proper, the other improper and metaphorical.

*Nep.* Are you bathed in luxury (*vivitisne lautè ?*) living here?

*Piso.* What do you mean by that? Do we wash ourselves (*an lavamur*)? Every day, hands and face, and indeed, frequently, for cleanliness of body is conducive to health and to nurture.

*Nep.* That is not what I ask—but whether you get food and drink to your mind?

26

*Piso.* We don't eat according to our desire, but according to the call of the palate.

*Nep.* I ask, if you eat, as you wish.

*Piso.* Certainly, forsooth, as hunger dictates. Who wishes to eat, eats; who does not wish, abstains.

*Nep.* Do you go from the table hungry?

*Piso.* By no means sated. For this is not wise. For it is the part of beasts, not men, to glut themselves. They say that a certain wise king never sat down to table without hunger, and never stood up sated.

*Nep.* What do you eat, then?

*Piso.* What there is.

*Nep.* Oh! I was thinking that you eat what you hadn't got! But what is there, then?

*Piso.* Troublesome questioner! What they give us.

*Nep.* But what do they give you, then?

## I. *Breakfast*

*Piso.* We have breakfast an hour and a half after we have got up.

*Nep.* When do you get up?

## II. *Lunch—Food—Drink*

*Piso.* Almost with the sun, for he is the leader of the Muses and the Muses are gracious to the dawn. Our early breakfast is a piece of coarse bread and some butter or some fruit as the time of the year supplies. For lunch, there are cooked vegetables or pottage in pottage-vessels, and

meat with relishes. Sometimes turnips, sometimes cabbages, starch-food, wheat-meal, or
rice. Then on fish-days, buttermilk from
butter which has been turned out in deep
dishes, with some cakes of bread, and a fresh
fish, if it can be bought fairly cheap in the
fish-market, or if not, a salt-fish, well soaked.
Then pease, or pulse, or lentils, or beans, or
lupines.

*Nep.* How much of these does each get?

*Piso.* Bread as much as he wishes; of viands as much
as is necessary not for satiety, but for nourish-
ment. For elaborate feasts, you must seek
elsewhere, not in the school, where the aim
is to form minds to the way of virtue.

*Nep.* What, then, do you drink?

### III. *Afternoon Meal*

*Piso.* Some drink fresh, clear water; others light beer;
some few, but only seldom, wine, well diluted.
The afternoon meal (*merenda*) or before-meal
consists of some bread and almonds or nuts,
dried figs and raisins; in summer, of pears,
apples, cherries, or plums.

### IV. *Chief Meal*

But when we go into the country for the
sake of our minds (recreation), then we have
milk, either fresh or congealed, fresh cheese,
cream, horse-beans soaked in lye, vine-leaves,
and anything else which the country house

affords. The chief meal begins with a salad
with closely - cut bits, sprinkled with salt,
moistened with drops of olive-oil, and with
vinegar poured on it.

*Nep.* Can you have nut or turnip oil?

*Piso.* Ugh! the unsavoury and unhealthy stuff!
Then there is in a great vessel a concoction of
mutton broth with sauce, and to it, dried plums,
roots, or herbs as supplements, and at times a
most savoury pie.

*Nep.* What sort of sauces do you have?

*Piso.* The best and wisest of sauces, hunger. Besides,
on appointed week-days we get roasted meat—
as a rule, veal; in spring sometimes, some
young kid. As an after-dish a little bit of
radish and cheese, not old and decayed, but
fresh cheese, which is more nourishing than
the old, pears, peaches, and quinces. On the
days on which no meat may be eaten, we have
eggs instead of meat, either broiled, fried, or
boiled, either singly by themselves or mingled
in one pan with vinegar or oil, not so much
poured on as dropped in; sometimes a little
fish, and nuts follow on cheese.

*Nep.* How much does every one get.

*Piso.* Two eggs and two nuts.


## V. *Sleeping Draught*

*Nep.* What! do you never have a sleeping draught
after supper?

*Piso.* Pretty often.

*Nep.* What do you have, I beg? for that is most delightful.

*Piso.* We prepare a banquet such as that of Syrus mentioned by Terence, or of one of the lordly people
mentioned by Athenaeus or of the like, of which
the record has been handed down in history.
Do you think us swine or men? What
stomach would preserve its soundness of
health if after four meals it were to add a
drinking-bout? Observe you are in a school,
not in an eating-house. For they say there
is nothing more ruinous to health than to
drink immediately before going to bed.

*Nep.* May I be allowed to be present at meal-time?

*Piso.* Certainly. Only I must first beg permission from
the teacher, who will, I am sure, give it without
difficulty, as is usual with him.

To take you to the banquet, without the
master's permission, would be ill breeding;
and he who should so bring you would draw
on himself from his fellow-disciples nothing
less than reproach and shame. Stop a
minute. Will you, sir, permit with your good
favour, that a certain boy known to me
should be present at our meal?

*Praec.* Certainly. There will be no harm in it.

*Piso.* Thank you. He whom thou seest there, who has
a napkin in place of a neck-cloth is the feast-
master of the dining-room (*architriclinus*) this
week—for here we have weekly feast-masters,
like kings.

*Feast-Master.* Lamia, what time is it?

*Lamia.* I have not heard the hours since the third, being intent on the composition of a letter. Florus will know this better than I, for he has not seen book or paper the whole of the afternoon.

*Florus.* This is friendly testimony, and if the teacher were angry, it would have great weight. But how couldst thou observe me, being immersed, as thou sayest, in the composition of a letter? Clearly ill-will has driven thee to telling a lie. I rejoice, indeed, that my enemy is held to be a liar. If after this he shall wish to say evil of me, such statements will not be believed.

*Feast-Master.* Can I not then, elsewhere, get to know as to the time? Anthrax, run across to St. Peter's and look at the time.

*Anthrax.* The pointer shows that it is now six o'clock.

## The Cups

*Feast-Master.* Six? Eh! boys, eh! Come, rouse yourselves; throw your books aside, even as the stag seeks a corner to hide his horns. Prepare the table, cover it, place seats, napkins, round and square plates, bread; fly, quicker than the word. Let not our teacher complain of our slowness. Bring beer, one of you; another, draw water from the well and place the cups. What is the meaning of this—bringing them so unclean? Take them back into the kitchen so that the maid may rub them clean and wipe them thoroughly, whereby they may be bright and shining.

*Piso.* Never will you accomplish this, so long as we have that monkey of a kitchen-maid. For she never dares to rub determinedly so as to clean, for she is afraid of her fingers. Nor does she rinse things more than once and that with tepid water.

*Arch.* Why don't you report this to the teacher?

*Piso.* It would be better to ask the housekeeper (*famulam atriensem*) for it is in her hands to change the kitchen-maids. But there is the teacher. Do you yourself wash these cups out, and rub them with a fig or nettle-leaf, or with sand and water, so that our schoolmaster to-day shall have no cause for blame.

*Praec.* Is all ready? Is there anything to delay you?

*Arch.* Nothing at all.

*Praec.* So that afterwards between the courses we need not have to make any break!

*Feast-Master.* Between the courses! Rather say *the* course and that a meagre one.

*Praec.* What are you murmuring?

*Feast-Master.* I say that you should sit down, that it is meal - time, and that the food will soon get spoilt!

*Praec.* You boys, wash your hands and mouth. Eh! what napkin is this? When did they clean themselves who wiped themselves dry on this? Run, fetch another cleaner than this. Let us sit down in our usual order. Is this the boy who is to be our guest?

*Piso.* Yes, this is he.

*Master.* Of what country is he?

*Piso.* A Fleming.

*Master.* Of what city in that province?

*Piso.* From Bruges.

*Master.* Let him sit in the seat close to you. Let every one take his knife and clean his bread, if there should stick any ashes or coal on the crust. Whose turn is it this week to say grace (*sacret mensam*)?

### Grace Before Meat

*Florus.* Feed our hearts with Thy love, O Christ, who through Thy goodness nourishest the lives of all living beings. Blessed be these Thy gifts to us who partake of them so that Thou who providest them may be blessed.[1] Amen.

*Master.* Sit as far apart as possible, so as not to press against one another's sides, since there is sufficient room for each. And you, Brugensian, have you a knife?

*Piso.* This is a wonder! A Fleming without a knife, and he, too, a Brugensian, where the best knives are made.

*Nep.* I don't need a knife. I can part my food into pieces by biting it with the teeth, and tear it into bits by my fingers.

*Usher.* They say that biting is very useful both for the gums and also for the surface of the teeth.

*Master.* Where didst thou receive early instruction in

---

[1] Pasce animos nostros Christe charitate tua, qui benignitate tua alis vitas animantium: sancta sint, Domine, haec tua munera nobis sumentibus, ut tu, qui ea largiris, sanctus es. Amen.

the Latin tongue, for thou appearest to me not badly taught?

*Nep.* At Bruges, under John Theodore Nervius.

*Master.* An industrious, learned, and honest man. Bruges is a most elegant city, but it is to be regretted that owing to the changing of the population from day to day, it is going down. When did you leave it?

*Nep.* Six days ago.

*Master.* When did you begin to study?

*Nep.* Three years ago.

*Master.* You have not got on badly.

*Nep.* Deservedly; for I have had a master I am not ashamed of.

*Master.* But what is *our Vives* doing?

*Nep.* They say that he is training as an athlete, yet not by athletics.

*Master.* What is the meaning of that?

*Nep.* He is always wrestling, but not bravely enough.

*Master.* With whom?

*Nep.* With his gout (*morbo articulari*).

*Master.* O mournful wrestler, which first of all attacks the feet.

*Usher.* Nay, rather cruel victor which fetters the whole body. But what are you doing? Why do you stop eating? You would seem to have come here not to eat, but to stare around. Let nobody during the meal disturb his cap lest any hair fall into the dishes. Why don't you treat your guest as a comrade? Nepotulus, I drink to you.

*Nep.* Sir, your toast is most welcome.

*Usher*. Empty your cup, since so meagre a draught remains in it.

*Nep*. This would be new to me.

*Praec*. What! not empty it? But you, Usher, what do you say? What have you new to give us at our meal?

*Grammatical Questions—1. On Genders. 2. On Tenses*

*Usher*. I say nothing indeed, but I have thought much during the last two hours on the art of grammar.

*Master*. And what of that now?

*Usher*. On very hidden things and the penetration of learning: first, why the grammarians have placed in their art three genders when there are merely two in nature? again, why nature does not produce things of the neuter gender as it does of the masculine and feminine? I cannot find out the cause of this great mystery. So, too, the philosophers say that there are three tenses, but our art demands five, therefore our art is outside the nature of things.

*Master*. Nay, rather thou art thyself outside of the nature of things, for art is in the nature of things.

*Usher*. If I am outside the nature of things, how can I eat this bread and meat, which are in the nature of things?

*Master*. Thou art so much the worse to belong to another nature whilst you eat what belongs to this our nature.

*Nep*. Παράφθεγμα ἀπροσδιόνυσον. I would wish another solution of my questions. Would that we had now some Palaemon or Varro who could resolve these questions.

*Master.* Why not rather another, an Aristotle or Plato? Have you not something further to say?

### Pronunciation

*Usher.* Yesterday I saw committed a crime of deepest dye (*scelus capitale*). The schoolmaster of the Straight Street (*vicus rectus*), who smells worse than a goat, and instructs his threepenny classes in his school, which abounds in dirt and filth, pronounced three or four times *volucres* with the accent on the penultimate. I indeed was astounded that the earth did not at once gulp him up.

*Praec.* What otherwise ought one to expect such a schoolmaster to say? He is in other parts of the grammatical rules thoroughly worn out (*detritus*). But you are disturbed over a very small matter and make a tragedy out of a comedy, or still more truly a farce.

*Usher.* I have finished my task. Now it is your turn. You now keep the conversation going.

*Praec.* I don't wish to give you the chance to answer me what I don't ask (παραφθέγγης). This broth is getting cold. Bring a table fire-pan. Heat it up a little before you dip your bread in it. This radish is not eatable, it is so tough —and so are the rootlets in the broth.

*Usher.* They certainly have not brought the toughness from the market, but they have acquired it here in our store-room in which the pantry is quite unsuited for provisions. I don't know why it is we always have brought to us here bones without marrow in them.

*Praec.* Bones have but little marrow in them at the new moon (*sub lunam silentem*).

*Usher.* What when it is full moon?

*Praec.* Then there is plenty.

*Usher.* But our bones have little, or more truly no, marrow.

*Praec.* It is not the moon that bereaves us of marrow but our Lamia. She has here put in too much pepper and ginger, and in the soup and particularly in the salad there is also too much mint, rock-parsley, sage, cole-wort, cress, hyssop. Nothing is more harmful to the bodies of boys and youths than foods which make the stomach hot.

*Arch.* What kinds of herbs then would you wish to be used for food?

*Praec.* Lettuce, garden-oxtongue, purslain, mixed with some rock-parsley.

### Manners at Table—The Clearing of the Table

Here, you, Gangolfus, don't wipe your lips with your hand or on your cuff, but wipe both lips and hands with your napkin, which has been provided you for the purpose. Don't touch the meat, except on that side which you are about to take yourself. You, Dromo, don't you observe that you are putting your coat-sleeves into the fat of the meat? If they are open, tuck them up to the shoulders. If they are not, turn them or fold them to the elbow. If they slip back again, fix them firm with a needle, or what would be still more suitable for you, with a thorn. You, delicate little lordling, you are reclining on the table. Where did you learn to do that? In some hog-stye? Eh! you there, put him a little cushion for him to lean on. Prefect of the table, see that the remains of the dinner don't get wasted. Put them away in the store-room. Take away first of all the salt-cellar, then the bread, then the dishes, plates, napkins, and lastly the table-cloth. Let each one clean his own knife and put it away in its sheath. You there, Cinciolus, don't scrape your teeth with your knife, for it is injurious. Make for yourself a tooth-pick of a feather or of a thin sharp piece of wood, and scrape gently, so as not to scar the gum or draw blood. Stand up all of you and wash your hands before thanks are returned. Move the table away, call the maid that she may sweep the floor with the broom. Let us thank Christ. Let him who said grace return thanks.

### Grace after the Meal

*Florus.* For this timely meal, we render Thee timely thanks, Lord Christ. Grant that we may for eternity render immortal thanks. Amen.

*Praec.* Now go and play, and have your talk, and walk about wherever you please, whilst the light permits.

# VIII

## GARRIENTES—*Students' Chatter*

NUGO, GRACULUS, TURDUS, BAMBALIO

In this dialogue Vives puts forth nineteen little narratives suited to the age of childhood and as it were the progymnasmata of eloquence. The names also of the interlocutors are neatly fabled.

*Nugo* is so called from *nugae*, as if a small retailer of trifles (*nugivendulus*).

*Graculus* and *Turdus* are feigned names from the loquacity of those birds. Compare the Proverbs, *Graculus graculo assidet* (one jackdaw resembles another),[1] *surdior turdo* (deafer than a thrush).

*Bambalio* is a man of worthlessness and of stammering speech as Cicero interprets it. Philip. 3. Compare the Proverb *Bambylius homo*.

## I. *Story of the Trunk*

*Nugo.* Let us sit on this trunk, and you, Graculus, on that stone facing us, so that without anything to hinder us we may observe all who pass by. We shall keep ourselves warm near this wall, which is excellently exposed to the sun. What a fine trunk is this and how enjoyable it is!

*Turd.* For us to sit on it!

*Nugo.* It must have been a very high and thick tree from which it was cut.

*Turd.* Such as there are in India.

*Grac.* How do you know! Have you been in India with the Spaniards?

[1] In John Conybeare's *Collection of Proverbs* (1580-1594) the following rendering is given: " One knave will kepe another companye, one pratteler wille with another, like will to like." *Letters and Exercises of John Conybeare*, p. 42. London: Henry Frowde, 1905.

*Turd.* As if one could know nothing of a district without having been in it! But I will give you my
authority. Pliny writes that trees in India
grow to such a height that a man cannot shoot
a dart over them, and the people there are not
to seek in shooting their arrows, as Vergil says.

*Nugo.* Pliny also says that a company of horsemen
could be hidden under the branches.

*Turd.* No one can wonder at that who considers the
rushes of that district, which the infirm people,
at any rate the rich, use to support them in
walking.

*Grac.* Eh! what hour is it?

## II. *The Hour-Bells*

*Nugo.* No hour at all, for the hour-bell is now thrown
down to the ground. Haven't you been to
see it?

*Grac.* I did not dare, for they say that it is dangerous.

*Nugo.* I have been there and saw no end of women with
child spring across the channel for the molten
metal, which is dug in the earth.

*Turd.* I heard that this was beneficial for them.

*Grac.* This is distaff philosophy, as they say, but I was
inquiring as to the hour.

## III. *The Timepiece*

*Nugo.* What need have you to know the time? If you
wish to do anything, while there is opportunity,
there is the time for it. But where is your
watch (*horologium viatorium*)?

*Grac.* I let it fall lately, when I was escaping the dog belonging to the gardener, whose plums I had plucked.

*Turd.* From the window I saw you running, but I could not see where you fled because the view was blocked by the fruit garden, which my mother has planted there, against the will of my father, and in spite of his many protests. But my mother, indeed, in the beginning was persistent in getting her own way, so that it could scarcely be borne.

*Nugo.* What is amiss with you? You are becoming silent.

*Turd.* I was weeping and said nothing, for what should I otherwise do when my dearest ones disagree? To be sure my mother ordered me to stand by her as she called lustily; but I had not the heart to mutter a word against my father. Therefore I was sent to school four days running without breakfast by my enraged mother, and she swore I was not her son, but had been changed by the nurse, for which she would have the nurse summoned before the *Praetor capitalis.*

*Nugo.* Who is the *Praetor capitalis?* Hasn't every *Praetor* got a head on?

*Turd.* How am I to know? So she said.

*Grac.* Look there! Who are those people with mantles, and armour for the legs.

## IV. *The French*

*Nugo.* They are Frenchmen.

*Grac.* What, is there then peace?

*Turd.* They said that there was to be war and a dire war too.

*Grac.* What are they carrying?

*Turd.* Wine.

*Nugo.* Then they will give pleasure to many.

*Grac.* Of a surety. For not only does wine cheer in drinking, but there is also the thought and recollection of it.

*Nugo.* At any rate for wine-drinkers. It matters nothing to me, for I drink water.

*Grac.* Then you will never write a good poem.


V. *The Deaf Woman*

*Turd.* Do you know that woman there?

*Grac.* No, who is she?

*Turd.* She has her ears stopped up against gossip.

*Grac.* Why so?

*Turd.* So as to hear nothing; because she hears ill of herself.[1]

*Nugo.* How many " hear ill of themselves " who have unstopped and normal ears?

*Turd.* I believe that it is to the point to quote the passage in Cicero's *Tusculanae Quaestiones*. M. Crassus was somewhat deaf—but what was worse, he "heard ill."

*Nugo.* There is no doubt that this must be traced back to slander. But, I say, Bambalio, have you found your *Tusculanae Quaestiones* ?

---

[1] *Audire male.* To have an evil reputation. Lewis and Short aptly quote from Milton's *Areopagitica :* " For which England hears ill abroad."

## VI. *The Lost Book*

*Bamb.* Yes, at the huckster's, but so interpolated that I did not at first recognise it.

*Nugo.* Who had stolen it?

*Bamb.* Vatinius. And may he be repaid for his misdeed!

*Grac.* Ah! that man with the hook-like and pitch-black hands! Never let such a man have access to your book-cases, nor to your manuscript-boxes if you wish all your things to be safe and sound. Don't you know that every one holds Vatinius for a thief of purses and he has been accused of thieving purses before the Principal (*gymnasiarcha*).

## VII. *The Twins*

*Nugo.* The sister of the girl there yesterday gave birth to twins.

*Grac.* What is there wonderful in that? A woman living in Salt Street at the Helmeted Lion six days ago had a triplet.

*Nugo.* Pliny says that there have been as many as seven at a birth.

*Turd.* Who of you has heard of the wife of the Count of Holland who is said to have had at a birth as many children as there are days in the year, owing to the curse of a certain beggar?

*Grac.* What was the story of this beggar?

*Turd.* This beggar was laden with children and begged an alms of the countess. But when she saw so many children, she drove the beggar away

by her reproaches, calling her a harlot. She
said she could not possibly have had from one
man so great a family. The innocent beggar
prayed the gods that as they knew she was
chaste and pure, they would give the countess
from her husband at one birth as many
children as there are days in the year. So it
happened, and the numerous posterity is
shown [1] in a certain town in that island to-day.

*Grac.* I will rather believe this than investigate it.

*Nugo.* All things are possible with God.

*Grac.* And, moreover, easy of accomplishment.

### VIII. *Mannius the Hunter*

*Nugo.* Don't you know that man there laden with nets
accompanied by dogs? He wears a summer
hat and soldier's boots, and rides on the lankest
of mules.

*Turd.* Isn't it Mannius the verse-maker?

*Nugo.* Clearly it is.

*Turd.* Why has he made such a metamorphosis?

### IX. *Curius the Dicer*

*Nugo.* From Minerva he has gone over to Diana, *i.e.*,
from a most honourable occupation to an empty
and foolish labour. His father had increased
his possessions by his ability in business.
He thinks his father's skill is a dishonour to
himself, and turns himself to keeping horses

---

[1] On a tombstone. Dr. Bröring quotes from Guicciardini,
*Belgicae Descriptio*, 1635, where an account is given of the tomb-
stone to a daughter of the Countess Mathilde of Holland in a
Cloister near the Hague.

and following the chase, having thought that not otherwise than by hunting can he acquire nobility of race. For if he were to do anything useful, he would not be held of noble family. Curius follows him to the hunt—with dice. He is a very accomplished man, a very well-known dice-player, who understands how to throw the dice in the right way for himself. At home he has for companion Tricongius.

*Turd.* Say rather an amphora.[1]

*Grac.* Or indeed a sponge.

*Nugo.* Better still, the driest sand of Africa.

*Bamb.* They say that he is always thirsty.

*Nugo.* Whether he is always thirsty or not, I don't know. But certainly he is always ready to drink.

### X. *The Nightingale and the Cuckoo*

*Bamb.* Listen, there is the nightingale!

*Grac.* Where is she?

*Bamb.* Don't you see her there, sitting on that branch? Listen how ardently she sings; and how she goes on and on!

*Nugo.* (As Martial says) *Flet philomela nefas.* (The nightingale weeps at injustice.)

*Grac.* What a wonder she carols so sweetly when she is away from Attica where the very waves of the sea dash upon the shore not without rhythm (*non sine numero*).

[1] *Amphora* is a measure for liquids. It was equal to six gallons seven pints. The *congius*, in the *Tri-congius*, was a measure of one-eighth of an *amphora*.

*Nugo.* Pliny observes that they sing with more exactitude when men are near them.

*Turd.* What is the reason for that?

*Nugo.* I will declare unto you the reason. The cuckoo and the nightingale sing at the same time, that is, from the middle of April till the end of May or thereabouts. These two birds once met in a contest of sweetness of song, when a judge was sought, and because it was a trial concerning sound, an ass seemed the most suitable for this decision, since he of all the animals had the longest ears. The ass rejected the nightingale, because he could not understand her harmony, and awarded the victory to the cuckoo. The nightingale appealed to men, and when she sees a man she immediately pours forth her song, and sings with zest so as to approve herself to him, so as to avenge the wrong which she received from the ass.

*Grac.* This is a subject worthy of a poet.


## XI. *Our Masters*

*Nugo.* Why, don't you think it worthy of a philosopher? Ask the question of our new masters from Paris.

*Grac.* Many of them are philosophers in their clothes, not in their brains.

*Nugo.* Why do you say on account of their dress? For you should rather say that they seem to be cooks or mule-drivers.

*Grac.* I say so because they wear clothes which are

clumsy, worn out, torn, muddy, dirty, and full
of lice in them.

*Nugo.* Why this almost constitutes them cynic philosophers!

*Grac.* Nay, they are rather *cimici* [1] but not what they
desire to seem, viz., *peripatetics*, for Aristotle,
the leader of this sect, was a most polished
man.   But I have long since bidden farewell
to philosophy, if I cannot any other way than
theirs become a philosopher.   For what is more
comely and worthy in a man than cleanliness
and a certain refinement in bearing and in
dress?   In   this   respect   I   consider   the
Lovanians are superior to the Parisians.

*Turd.* But don't you think that too much attention to
cleanliness and elegance is a hindrance to
studies?

*Grac.* I certainly believe in cleanliness, but I don't
think there should be an anxious and morose
absorption in it.

*Nugo.* Do you then condemn elegance, on which Laurentius Valla has written so diffusely and which
our teachers so diligently commend to us?
There is an elegance, *e.g.*, of words, in speaking, and there is an elegance of clothes in
dressing.

*Turd.* Do you know what was told me by the letter-
carrier at Louvain?

*Nugo.* What was that?

*Turd.* That Clodius fell in love madly with some girl
and Lusco transferred himself from letters to

[1] *I.e.* of the nature of bugs.

merchandise, that is, from horseback to mule-back.

*Nugo.* What do I hear?

## XII. *Clodius the Lover*

*Turd.* You all knew Clodius, full of vigour, rubicund, well-clothed, cheerful, with shining countenance, affable, genial teller of stories. Now it is said of him that he is without vigour, bloodless, of pallid colour, sallow, witless, wild-looking, stern, taciturn, one who shuns the light and human society. No one who knew him formerly would now recognise him.

*Nugo.* O wretched young man! Whence has this evil befallen him?

*Turd.* He is in love.

*Nugo.* But whence his love?

*Turd.* As far as I could gather from the speech of the letter-carrier he had given up solid and serious studies and had devoted himself entirely to the looser Latin poets—those of the vernacular; thence he got the first preparation of his mind. So that if by any means any spark of fire, however slight it might be, should fall on him he was as kindling-wood ready for it and would flare up suddenly like lit flax. So he gave himself up to sleep and idleness.

*Nugo.* What need is there further to relate more or greater causes of his falling in love?

*Turd.* Now he is beside himself, going about here, there, and everywhere alone, but always either silent, or singing something and dancing, and writing verses in the vernacular.

*Nugo.* Which, forsooth, his Lycoris herself may read.

*Grac.* O Christ, preserve our hearts from so pernicious a disease!

*Turd.* Unless I am deceived as to the character of Clodius, he will return some time to a better and more fruitful life. His mind wanders into the foreign lands of evil; it does not take up its residence in them.

### XIII. *Lusco the Merchant*

*Grac.* And that other one—what is the kind of commerce in which he engages?

*Turd.* He has sent his father a letter written in a weeping strain concerning the sad state of his studies. The letter-carrier himself read the letter since it was left open. The father, a man impervious to culture (*crassae Minervae*), has handed him over from MSS. to wools, cloths, dyes, pepper, ginger, and cinnamon. Now girt as to his arms, wonderfully diligent and sedulous in his odorous shop, he invites his customers, receives them blandly, climbs up and comes down most unsafe ladders, produces his goods, shows them this way and that, tells lies, perjures himself. Everything is easier to him than studying.

*Nugo.* From a boy I have known him intent on business, and to delight in money, and so he has held business in higher esteem than letters, and he

has preferred filthy lucre to the excellency of
erudition.   Some time he will repent it.

*Turd.* But too late!

*Nugo.* Without doubt.  May he take care that it does
not happen to him as it did to his cousin.

*Turd.* Which?


## XIV. *Antony the " Cook "*

*Nugo.* Antonius in Fruit Lane, near the Three Jack-
daws.   Haven't you heard that in a former
year he " cooked "? [1]

*Grac.* What did he cook, please?   Is this so great an
evil?   Doesn't it go on in every kitchen daily?

*Turd.* He " cooked " his accounts (*rem decoxit*).

*Grac.* What accounts?

*Turd.* His business with others, and couldn't meet his
creditors.

*Grac.* Hasn't he paid back his creditors?

*Turd.* He has betaken himself to a place of retreat, and
made over his books one by one at a quarter
of their cost price.

*Grac.* Is this what you call " cooking," when nothing
could be more raw.   But how did he lose the
money?

*Turd.* I have heard lately from his father with regard
to that, but I have not yet fully understood
the matter.   The father said that he had made
most prodigal borrowings, which would skin
him and swallow him up to the bones.

---

[1] *Decoxisse* from *decoquere*—which means both to cook and to
become bankrupt.

*Grac.* What do you mean by " borrowings " and what
by " skinning "?

*Turd.* I don't quite know, but I believe it has something to do with theft.

## XV. *The Tumbler*

*Nugo.* Do you see, there, that fat man? You would
scarcely think it possible to move him. Yet
he is a tumbler and rope-dancer (*funambulus*).

*Grac.* Ah! be quiet! You are saying something which
is incredible.

*Turd.* He does not indeed dance with his body, but he
makes drinking-cups dance.

*Grac.* Did the letter-carrier bring any news of our
companions?

## XVI. *Hermogenes*

*Turd.* Yes, concerning Hermogenes, who in all our contests always bore away the chief prizes. By
an astounding change from being a man of
the highest ability and learning (as his time of
life brought about) suddenly he has become
most sluggish and boorish.

*Nugo.* Such a change I have often seen happen with
certain keen-witted men.

*Bamb.* They say that this happens when the sharpness
of the wit is not really genuine, like a lancet
whose edge is easily blunted, especially if it is
used to cut anything a little too hard.

*Grac.* What, is there an edge in wits, even as there is in
steel?

*Bamb.* I don't know. I have often seen steel, but
never have I seen a man's wits.


## XVII. *The Boorish Youth*

*Nugo.* What has become of that young countryman
(*paganus*) who some months ago on his arrival
entertained us with a lunch consisting of
delicacies brought from the country, after
whom the teacher has sent four slave-catchers
to bring him back from his flight? He was
rather a handsome fellow!

*Turd.* He has become a delightful ass! My aunt's
maid-servant, who is his cousin, met him
lately in his village, with bare head, uncombed,
shaggy, and bristly, with wooden shoes and a
poor, rough coat, selling in a public square
paper pictures and horn books, and singing
new songs before a circle of sightseers.

*Grac.* Yet he must be a man sprung from a distinguished family.

*Turd.* Why so?

*Grac.* Since his father is of the race of the Coclites.

*Nugo.* That name does not so much argue a man of
noble family as a thrower of the dart. He
will take his aim easily.

*Turd.* Or it betokens a carpenter who directs his red-
chalk with one eye.

*Nugo.* That boy has never pleased me, nor has he ever
disclosed to me any sign of ability.

*Grac.* How so?

### XVIII. *The Man with the Neck Chain*

*Nugo.* Because he never loved studies, nor showed any
reverence for his teacher. This is the clearest
proof of a lost mind. Then, too, he ridiculed
old men and mocked at the unfortunate.
But who is that man clothed in silk, adorned
with neck-chain and with gold decorations?

*Grac.* He is of a renowned race, and has a mother a
most noble and fruitful mother.

*Nugo.* Who is she?

*Grac.* The earth,[1] and you will scarcely believe what
delights he always has. You would say he
was a little child up to now in the cradle, cry-
ing for his rattle.

*Nugo.* And yet the down begins to creep over his cheeks.


### XIX. *The Overseer of Studies*

*Bamb.* Ah! the overseer (*observator*) is coming. Get
ready your books, open them, and begin to
turn over the pages and read them.

There has not been for many weeks a more
zealous overseer, one who would rejoice so
much to pass on charges against any one to the
master.

*Bamb.* Would that at least he would accuse us of our
real faults, but for the most part he brings false
witness against us.

---

[1] Dr. Bröring quotes from Erasmus's *Adages*, Chil. I. Cent. viii.
Prov. 86, to show that formerly men of obscure birth were
termed *terrae filii*.

*Nugo.* Let that saying of Horace be a wall of brass to us:

> Nihil conscire sibi, nulla pallescere culpa.

But be quiet! I will immediately put him to rout.

*Observ.* What do you say, Vacia?

*Nugo.* What do you say, Vatrax?

*Observ.* What do you say, Batrachomyomachia? But, joking aside, what are you doing here?

*Nugo.* What are we doing? What are good scholars and students always doing? We are reading, learning, disputing. Tell us, please, most charming creature,[1] what is the meaning of that passage in Vergil's *Eclogues:*

> . . . transversa tuentibus hirquis.

*Observ.* You do well; proceed with your studies as it behoves young men of good abilities. I have now other business in hand. Farewell.

*Nugo.* We have had sufficient trifling. Let us get back to school. But first let us read over again what the teacher explained, so that we learn something, and give him pleasure, and so that he may approve of us—which must be in our prayers as much as it is in those of the father of each of us.

[1] *Capitulum lepidissimum*—a term of endearment used by Terence.

# IX

## ITER ET EQUUS—*Journey on Horseback*

### Philippus, Misippus, Misospudus, Planetes

In this dialogue are contained those matters that pertain to horses and peregrinations, concerning which see as a whole, Grapaldus, lib. 1, cap. 8, and Volaterranus, lib. 25, philologiae. We place the kinds one by one, according to their nomenclature, primarily for the sake of boys.

*Lupatum*, ein scharpff Gebisz.
*Frenum*, ein Zaum.
*Orea*, der Riem unter dem Maul.
*Aurea*, der Riem über die Ohren.
*Antilena*, der Brustriem.
*Postilena*, der hinder Riem.   Hinderbug.
*Ephippium*, Sattel.
*Stapes vel stapeda*, Steigreiff.
*Habena*, Zügel.
*Calcar*, Spor.

### Genera Equorum

*Asturco gradarius, tollutarius, tieldo*, ein Zelter.
*Mannus*, ein kleines Rösslein.
*Cantherius*, ein Mönch.
*Succussator*, ein barttrabander Gaul.
*Vector sen ephippiarius*, Reitrosz.
*Clitellarius*, Saumrosz.
*Jugalis, helciarius*, Ziehrosz. Wagenrosz. Kummetrosz.
*Dorsualis*, Müllerrosz, das auff dem Rücke trägt.
*Meritorius*, Lehenrosz.   Drei Plappert Rosz.

### Currus

| Species | Rheda, ein Karz. |
| | Sarracum, Lastwagen. Stein. Wagen. |

| Partes | Rotae, Reder. |
| | Temo, Deichsel. |
| | Canthi, Radschinnen. |

The names of the interlocutors are suitably framed. Misippus, the hater of horses, μισῶν τοὺς ἵππους; Philippus, the lover of horses, φιλῶν τοὺς ἵππους; Misospudus, the hater of studies (*osor studiorum*), μισων τῶν σπυδίων; Planetes erro, vagus, planus, ein Landstreicher, from πλανάομαι, erro, vagor.

*Phil.* Wouldn't you like us to set out for Boulogne along the Seine, to cheer our minds?

*Misi. and Miso.* There is nothing we should like better, especially on a mild day like this, without a sound of wind, and when, again, we are having a holiday from school.

*Phil.* Why are you not at work to-day?

*Miso.* Because Pandulfus is going to make all the masters drunk with a great luncheon in honour of his laurels in obtaining his mastership.

*Plan.* Oh! what a lot they will drink!

*Miso.* Much more than will satisfy thirst.

*Misi.* I have an Asturian horse.

*Phil.* And I have a hired horse which I have got from a one-eyed rogue.

*Miso.* Planetes and I will go in a travelling carriage; the rest, if it seems good to them, shall follow us on foot, or by strength of arms push a boat against the current of the stream.

*Phil.* Rather let it be dragged along by horses.

*Miso.* As you please (*ut erit cordi*), for we choose to take the journey on foot.

*Phil.* Eh! boy, bridle my horse and saddle him! Why, in the name of mischief, are you putting on the little steed so sharp-toothed a curb? Give him rather that light little curb with the knobs.

*Boy.* Alas! he has neither bit nor bridle.

*Phil.* If I knew who had broken them, I would break him!

*Misi.* What are you saying in your agitation?

*Phil.* Put in bread for a meal. Get it where you can, conveniently.

*Boy.* Certainly, whilst you are at your school classes. You want both horses and their equipment!

*Phil.* Supply, then, what is lacking out of this cord.

*Boy.* It will look unsightly.

*Phil.* Go, fool, who will see us when we get out of the town?

*Boy.* The body-band is also in two.

*Phil.* Mend it with some straps.

*Boy.* It has no tail-band.

*Phil.* There is no need for it.

*Plan.* A great and experienced horseman! Why, the the saddle will slide on to his neck and the horse will shoot you over his head.

*Phil.* What is that to me? The road is muddy rather than stony. I shall take my fill of dirt, but none of my blood will be spilt. If all these preparations have to be made, we shall not set forth from this place before the evening. Bring a horse of some kind, whatever his trappings may be.

*Boy.* Here he is, ready. Mount him. Eh! what are you doing, putting your right foot first into the stirrup?

*Phil.* What am I to do then?

*Boy.* Why, the left, and hold the reins in your left hand; with the right hand take this switch, which will serve in place of spurs.

*Phil.* I don't need it.   My heels will do for spurs.

*Boy.* You see Jubellius Taurea, or is it Asellus who entered into a struggle with that famous steed.[1]

*Phil.* Have done with your glib stories!   Where are the others?

*Boy.* Off you go!   I will accompany you on foot.

*Misi.* Most abominable, jolting horse.   The beast will break all my bones before we reach the town.

*Phil.* What, in the name of evil, is that horse-covering? It is a pack-saddle, I believe.

*Misi.* Surely not.

*Phil.* How much for it?   What's its price?

*Misi.* Fourteen Turonic[2] sesterces.

*Phil.* I wouldn't give as much for the horse himself with his fodder and trappings.   It seems to me to be neither a draught horse, nor a horse for riding, but a beast of burden, ready for the pack-saddle, or for the yoke, or to carry goods on its back.   Note, I beg, how it constantly stumbles.   It would trip up over a piece of paper, or a stalk of straw spread out on its way.

*Misi.* What do you say of it?   It is as yet a foal.   But chatter on as you like.   Do you see this horse? He, whatever he may be, is going to carry me, or I him.

*Boy.* The poor animal has a very tender hoof.

---

[1] Freigius notes that Jubellius Taurea was by far the strongest horse of the Campanians, whilst Claudius Asellus was a horseman of equally renowned horsemanship.   The steed challenged the rider to a contest.   *See* Livy, Bk. 3, Decad. 3.

[2] Of the town of Tours, in France.

*Phil.* What, then, did the one-eyed man so carefully warn you about when he handed the horse over to you?

*Misi.* He begged, in the most amiable manner, that the two of us should not sit on the beast, one on the saddle and the other on the buttocks, and that I should have him carefully covered when he was put in the stable.

*Boy.* The poor horse surely needs covering when he has his sides of raw flesh.

*Phil.* What are you doing? Are you not getting into the carriage?

*Plan.* You speak to the point. The driver now demands as much again as what we agreed to.

*Phil.* It is easy to deal with drivers and boatmen; they will do everything to your satisfaction. They tell you you will accomplish everything. This kind of man is soft, gentle, obliging, courteous, respectful. Drivers are the scum of the earth, the boatmen the scum of the sea. Give him the half of what he asks.

*Boy.* What time do you suppose it is already?

*Phil.* Guessing by the sun, I should say past ten o'clock.

*Boy.* Mid-day is near.

*Phil.* Fancy! Eh! Misippus, let us get along. Follow who can! We shall be found at the " Red Hat," *i.e.*, the hostelry situated opposite the royal pyramid, not far from the house of the Curio.[1]

*Misi.* Which way shall we go?

[1] It is explained by Vives, as a note in the margin, that Curio is the priest of the parish, commonly called curate.

*Phil.* Through the Marcelline Gate, on the right. It
is a simple and straight road.

*Misi.* Nay, let us take this lane. It is a pleasant and
quiet way.

*Phil.* By no means. Nothing is easier and safer than
the high road, for by cross roads we shall lose
our friends, especially since that way, if my
memory does not fail me, is full of windings
and turnings.

*Misi.* Who are those men with spears? They seem to
be soldiers from the mercenary troops.

*Phil.* What must we do?

*Misi.* Let us turn back, so that we don't get robbed.

*Phil.* Let us go forward, for on horseback we shall
easily escape them, by running through the
fields.

*Misi.* What if they have got handcuffs with them!

*Phil.* I see nothing of the sort, but only long lances.

*Misi.* Come nearer, boy.

*Boy.* What's amiss?

*Misi.* Don't you see those Germans?

*Boy.* Which?

*Misi.* Those people coming this way against us.

*Boy.* They are German [1] sure enough, but two Parisian
peasants with their sticks.

*Misi.* Yes, certainly, that is so. A blessing on you!
You have restored my courage and vitality.
But where are Misospudus and Planetes?

*Boy.* The driver, enraged at not getting what he had
demanded, drove them on a lumpy road.

---

[1] As Dr. Bröring remarks, " German " is used in the sense of
" brethren."

The horses, in struggling with all their might to drag the wheels as they stuck in the deep mud, broke in pieces the pole of the carriage and the horse-collars. Then the tyres, together with the nails, were torn off. The reckless driver, with blind rage, had put the brake on the wheel. He is now angrily repairing the damage and blaspheming all the gods, and cursing the passengers with the most terrible imprecations.

*Phil.* May his curses recoil on his own head!

*Boy.* I think they will leave the carriage behind and get into a cart, which is going, unladen, to Boulogne. Glaucus and Diomedes had got on a boat, but the boatman declared that against this wind they could not make way with their oars and poles. Also they say that the horses which pull boats up the stream are all at work, so I know not by what means the boat could be drawn. So they have not yet loosened the stern-rope.

*Phil.* Is there any news as to the boat fare?

*Plan.* Absolutely none.

*Phil.* That is extraordinary. I guess what will happen. They won't reach Boulogne before nightfall.

*Misi.* What of that! Let us take all to-morrow for refreshing our minds. But look how softly the river flows by! What a delightful murmur there is of the full crystal water amongst the golden rocks! Do you hear the nightingale and the goldfinch? Of a truth, the country round Paris is most delightful!

*Phil.* What sight can be equal to this? How placidly the Seine flows in its current, how that small ship with its full sail before a favourable breeze is borne along! It is marvellous how minds are restored by all these things. Oh, how the meadow is clothed as by magic art.

*Misi.* And, moreover, by what a marvellous Artist!

*Phil.* What a sweet scent is exhaled!

*Misi.* Here, here; bend to the left so as to escape the thickest of mud, in which thy steed at once would lose his hoof. How different this field is from the next, covered over with dirt, squalid, withered, bristling thick with straws, and armed with thorns.

*Boy.* Don't you see that the field is covered with the waste from the river? and elsewhere it is fruitful.

Hyberno pulvere, verno luto, magna farra Camille metes.[1]

*Phil.* Please, sing some verses, as you are wont to do.

*Misi.* With pleasure.

Felix ille animi, divisque simillimus ipsis,
Quem non mendaci resplendens gloria fuco
Sollicitat, non fastosi mala gaudia luxus:
Sed tacitos sinit ire dies, et paupere culta
Exigit innocuae tranquilla silentia vitae.[2]

---

[1] With dust in winter and mud in spring, you will reap great grain, Camillus. Macrobius, *Satur.* v. 20; cf. Vergil, *Georgics*, i. 101.

[2] Happy is the man in his heart, and approaching to the happiness of the gods themselves, whom glory does not agitate, dazzling with its lying gloss, nor the evil allurements of haughty luxury, but who lets the days pass peacefully by and silently, and with the labour of the poor man wins the peace of the blameless life.

*Phil.* Most elegant and matterful verses, whose are they, I beg?

*Misi.* Don't you know?

*Phil.* No.

*Misi.* They are by Angelus Politian.

*Phil.* I should have taken them to be from the classics. They have the grace of antiquity. I suspect we have lost our way!

*Misi.* Ah! good sir, which is the way to Boulogne?

*Rustic.* You are going out of the way. Turn your beasts to the cross-roads and strike the way there where the river bends. On it you cannot get wrong. The road is straight and plain up to the old oak, then you turn quickly on this side (pointing with his hand).

*Misi.* We are grateful.

*Rustic.* May God lead you!

*Misi.* I would rather run on foot than be shaken as I am by this horse.

*Phil.* You will have so much the greater appetite.

*Misi.* I shall, on the contrary, be able to eat nothing, so weary and exhausted I am in all my body. I would rather go to bed than ask for anything to eat.

*Phil.* Sit down, with knees drawn together, and not stretched apart. You will feel weariness the less.

*Misi.* That is the custom of women. I would do it were I not afraid of the laughter and grimaces of passers by.

*Boy.* Stop a moment, Philip, until the smith here has

shod thy horse, whose shoe on the right foot has become loose.

*Misi.* Nay, rather let us stay here, so that if the inn is closed we may sleep out in the open air.

*Phil.* What is that? Under the open sky? Would it not be more excellent than in a closed room? It would be a more serious matter for us to have to go without a meal.

# X

## SCRIPTIO—*Writing*

### Manricus, Mendoza, the Teacher

As, above, in the fifth dialogue, Vives taught the method of reading, so here he explains in an elegant manner the method of writing. For it is no small honour for a learned man to form his letters skilfully. But he adds the praise of correct writing and various kinds of writing, also he writes somewhat on pens and their preparation, and concerning different kinds of paper and other adjuncts of writing.

*Manr.* Were you present to-day when the oration on the usefulness of writing was delivered?

*Mend.* Where?

*Manr.* In the lecture-room of Antonius Nebrissensis.

*Mend.* No, but do you recount what took place, if anything of it remains in your memory.

*Manr.* What am I to recount? He said so many things that almost everything has fallen from my mind.

*Mend.* Then it has happened to you what Quintilian said of the vessels with narrow neck, viz., that they spit out the supply of liquid when it is poured down on them; but if it is instilled slowly they receive it. But haven't you retained anything of it exactly?

*Manr.* Almost nothing.

*Mend.* Then at least something.

*Manr.* Very, very little.

*Mend.* Then communicate this very, very little to me.

### I. *The Usefulness of Writing*

*Manr.* First of all he said that it was thoroughly wonderful that you can comprise so great a variety of human sounds within so few written characters. Then, that absent friends are able to talk to one another by the aid of letters. He added that nothing seemed more marvellous in these islands recently discovered by the munificence of our kings, whence indeed gold is brought, than that men should be able to open up to one another what they think from a long distance by a piece of paper being sent with black stains marked on it. For the question was asked, Whether paper knew how to speak? He also said this, that, and many other things which I have forgotten.

*Mend.* How long did he speak?

*Manr.* Two hours.

*Mend.* And from so long an oration have you committed to memory so slight a portion as what you have just said?

*Manr.* I have indeed *committed* it to the charge of my memory, but my memory would not keep it all.

*Mend.* Clearly you have the wide-mouthed jar of the daughters of Danaus.

*Manr.* Nay, I have received the oration into a sieve, not into a jar at all.

*Mend.* We will summon some one who will bring back to memory those points which you have forgotten.

*Manr.* Wait a bit! for I am seeking to recall something by thinking it over. Now I have it.

*Mend.* Speak it out, then! Why didn't you take notes?

*Manr.* I hadn't a pen at hand.

*Mend.* Not even a writing-tablet?

*Manr.* Not even a writing-tablet.

*Mend.* Now tell on.

*Manr.* I have lost it again; you have shaken it out of mind by interrupting so disagreeably.

*Mend.* What, so soon!

*Manr.* Now it comes back to me. He stated on the authority of some writer (I don't know who it was) that nothing is more fitted as a help to great erudition than to write clearly and quickly.

*Mend.* Who was the writer quoted?

*Manr.* I have often heard his name, but it has escaped my memory.

### Nobles

*Mend.* As have the other things! But the crowd of our nobility do not follow the precept (as to the value of writing), for they think it is a fine and becoming thing not to know how to form their letters. You would say their writing was the scratching of hens, and unless you were warned beforehand whose hand it was, you would never guess.

*Manr.* And for this reason you see how thick-headed men are, how foolish, and imbued with corrupt prejudices.

*Mend.* What are the common run of people, if the nobles are so skilless? or are the classes little different from each other?

*Manr.* Because the common people are not distinguished by their clothes and possessions, they are the more separated by their life and sound judgment in their affairs.

*Mend.* Do you mean that to vindicate ourselves from the charge of vulgar ignorance we must give ourselves up to the practice of writing?

*Manr.* I don't know how it is inborn in me to plough out my letters so distortedly, so unequally and confusedly.

*Mend.* You have this tendency from your noble birth. Practise yourself—habit will change even what you think to be inborn in you.

## II. *The Writing-master*

*Manr.* But where does he (the writing-master) live?

*Mend.* Don't seek that from me, for I did not hear the man, nor see him, while I understood that you heard him. You would like everything to be brought to your mouth, chewed beforehand.

*Manr.* Now I remember he said he rented a house near the church of SS. Justus and Pastor.

*Mend.* So he is our neighbour. Let us go.

*Manr.* Eh, boy! where is the teacher?

*Boy.* In that room there!

*Manr.* What is he doing?

*Boy.* He is teaching some pupils.

*Manr.* Tell him that there stand before his doors some who have come to be taught by him.

*Teacher*. Who are these boys? What do they want?

*Boy*. They desire conference with you.

*Teacher*. Admit them straight to me.

*Manr. and Mend*. We wish you health and all prosperity, teacher.

*Teacher*. And I, in my turn, wish you a happy entrance here. May Christ preserve you! What is it? What do you wish?

*Manr*. To be taught by you in that art which you profess, if only you have time and are willing.

*Teacher*. Certainly, you ought to be boys highly educated, for so you speak and desire with modest mouths. Now, so much the more since a blush has spread over your whole face. Have confidence, my boys, for that is the colour of virtue. What are your names?

*Manr*. Manricus and Mendoza.

### True Nobility

*Teacher*. The names themselves are evidence of noble education and generous minds. But first then, you will be truly noble if you cultivate your minds by those arts which are especially most worthy of your renowned families. How much wiser you are than that multitude of nobles who hope that they are going to be esteemed as better born in proportion as they are ignorant of the art of writing. But this is scarcely to be wondered at, since this conviction has taken hold of the stupid nobles that nothing is more mean or vile than to pursue knowledge in anything. And therefore it is to be seen that they sign their names to their letters, composed by their secretaries, in a manner that makes them impossible to be read; nor do you know from whom the letter is sent to you, if it is not first told you by the letter-carrier, or unless you know the seal.

*Manr.* Over this Mendoza and I have grieved already.

*Teacher.* But have you come here armed?

*Manr.* Not at all, good teacher, we should have been beaten by our teachers if we had dared to merely look at arms, at our age, let alone to touch them.

*Teacher.* Ah, ah! I don't speak of the arms of blood-shedding, but of writing-weapons, which are necessary for our purpose. Have you a quill-sheath together with quills in it?

*Mend.* What is a quill-sheath? Is it the same as we call a writing-reed case?

### III. *Modes of Writing*

*Teacher.* It is. For the men of antiquity were accustomed to write with styles. Styles were followed by reeds, especially Nile reeds. The Agarenes (*i.e.* the Saracens), if you have seen them, write with reeds from right to left, as do almost all the nations in the East. Europe followed Greece, and, on the contrary, writes from the left to the right.

*Manr.* And also the Latins?

*Teacher.* The Latins also, my sons, but they have their origin from the Greeks. Formerly the ancient Latins wrote on parchment which was called palimpsist, because the writing could be wiped out again, and only on one side, for those books written on both sides were called Opistographi. Such was that *Orestes* of Juvenal which was written on the back of a written sheet and not brought to an end. But as to these matters I will speak some other time; now those which press. We write with goose quills, though some use hen's quills. Your quills there are particularly useful, for they have an ample, shining, and firm opening. Take off the little feathers with a knife and cut off something from the top. If they have any roughness, scrape it off, for the smooth ones are better fitted for use.

*Manr.* I never use any unless they are stripped of feathers, and shine, but my instructor taught me how to make them smooth by saliva and by rubbing on the under-side of the coat or stockings.

*Teacher.* Seasonable counsel!

*Mend.* Teach us how to make our quills.

## IV. *The Making of (Quill) Pens*

*Teacher.* First of all, cleave the head on both sides, so that it is split into two. Then whilst you carefully guide the knife, make a cutting on the upper part which is called the *crena* or notch. Then make quite equal the two little feet (*pedunculos*), or if you prefer to call them the little legs (*cruscula*); so, nevertheless, that the right one on which the pen rests in writing may be higher, but the difference ought to be scarcely perceptible. If you wish to press the pen on the paper somewhat firmly, hold it with three fingers; but if you are writing more quickly, with two, the thumb and the fore-finger, after the Italian fashion. For the middle finger rather checks the course and hinders it from proceeding too quickly, instead of helping it forward.

*Manr.* Reach me the ink vessel.

*Mend.* Ah! I have let the ink horn fall, whilst coming here.

### V. *Ink*

*Teacher.* Boy, bring me that two-handled ink flask, and let us pour from it into this little leaden mortar.

*Mend.* Without a sponge!

*Teacher.* You get the ink thus more flowingly and easily into the pen. For if you dip the pen into cotton, or silk-thread, or linen, some fibre or fluff adheres to the nib. The drawing of this out causes a delay in writing. Or if you don't draw it out, you will make blurs rather than letters (*lituras verius quam literas*).

*Mend.* As my companions advised, I put in either Maltese linen-cloth or thin, fine silk.

*Teacher.* That is certainly more satisfactory. However, it is much better to pour ink only into a little mortar which stands firmly, for that can be carried about; for this, of course, a sponge is necessary. Have you also paper?

## VI. *Paper*

*Mend.* I have this.

*Teacher.* It is too rough, and such as would check the pen so that it would not run without being hindered, and this is a nuisance for studies. For whilst you are struggling with roughness of paper, many things which should be written down slip from the mind. Leave this kind of paper, wide, thick, hard, rough, for the printers of books, for it is so called (*libraria*) because from it books are made to last for a very long time. For daily use, don't get great Augustan or Imperial paper, which is named Hieratica because employed for sacred matters, such as you see in books used in sacred edifices. Get for your own use the best letter-paper from Italy, very thin and firm, or even that common sort brought over from France, and especially that which you will find for sale in single blocks at twopence each (*nummis octonis*). In addition, the linden-tree paper, either of the kinds of paper called Emporetica,[1] which we call blotting paper (*bibula*), should be in reserve (*pro corollario*).

*Mend.* What do these words mean, for I have often wondered?

*Teacher.* *Emporetica* comes from the Greek and means paper used for wrapping goods in, and *bibula* is so called because it absorbs ink, so that you don't need bran, or sand, or dust scraped from

---

[1] *I.e.*, shop packing-paper.

a wall. But best of all is when the letters dry up of themselves, for by that method they last so much longer. But you will find it useful to place *Emporetica* paper under your hand so that you may not stain the whiteness of the writing-paper by sweat or dirt.

## VII. *The Copy*

*Manr.* Now give us a copy, if it seems good to you.

*Teacher.* First the A B C, then syllables, then words joined together in this fashion. Learn, boy, those·things by which you may become wiser, and thence happier. Sounds are the symbols of minds amongst people in one another's presence; letters, the symbols between those who are absent from one another. Imitate these copies and come here after lunch, or even to-morrow, so that I may correct your writing.

*Manr.* We will do so. In the meantime we commend you to Christ.

*Teacher.* And I, you, the same.

*Mend.* Let us go apart from our friends, so that we may reflect without interruption on what we have heard from the teacher.

*Manr.* Agreed! Let us do so!

*Mend.* We have come to the place we want. Let us sit down on these stones.

*Manr.* Yes, as long as we are out of the sun.

*Mend.* Quick! a half-sheet of paper, which I will return to you to-morrow.

*Manr.* Will this small bit be sufficient?

*Mend.* Alas! it won't take six lines, especially of such writing as mine.

*Manr.* Write on both sides and make the lines more crowded together. What need have you to leave such big spaces between the lines?

*Mend.* I? I make scarcely any space. For these letters of mine touch one another both above and beneath, especially those which have long heads or feet, such as *b* and *p*. But what are you doing? Have you already ploughed out two lines? and how elegant they are! except that they are crooked.

*Manr.* You write, yourself, and be quiet!

*Mend.* Certainly with this pen and ink I can by no means write.

*Manr.* How is that?

*Mend.* Don't you see that the pen besprinkles the paper with ink outside the letters?

*Manr.* My ink is so thick that you would think it was lime. Look there, how it sticks on the top of the nib and won't flow down so as to form the letters. But we will soon remedy both the inconveniences. Cut off from the top of the pen with your knife so much that it collects what is wanted for the letters; I will instil some drops of water into the ink so as to make it flow more easily. The best thing would be vinegar, if you had it at hand, for this immediately dilutes the thick ink.

*Mend.* True, but there is the danger lest its acidity enters into the paper.

*Manr.* You needn't fear any such danger; this paper is best of all in preventing ink from flowing.

*Mend.* The extreme edges of this paper of yours are unequal, wrinkled, and rough.

*Manr.* Then apply the shears to the margin of the paper, for then it will seem more elegant, or write only outside the rough parts. The slightest obstacles seem to you to be a great hindrance to prevent you going on. Whatever you have under your hand, put it on one side.

*Mend.* Let us now go back to the teacher.

*Manr.* Does it seem to you to be time already?

*Mend.* I fear lest the time has already passed by, for he has lunch early.

*Manr.* Let us go. You enter first, for you have less timidity.

*Mend.* Nay, rather you, for you have less impudence.

*Manr.* See that no one goes out from his house and catches us here, joking and frolicking. Let us knock at the door with the knocker-ring, although the door is open, for this would be more courteous. (Tat-tat.)

*Boy.* Who is there? Come straight in, whoever you are!

*Manr.* It is we. Where is the teacher?

*Boy.* In his room.

*Mend.* May all things befall you propitiously, teacher!

*Teacher.* You have come seasonably.

*Mend.* We have imitated your copy five or six times on this paper and bring our work to you to have it corrected.

*What should be Avoided in Writing*

*Teacher.* You have done rightly. Show it. In the future let there be a greater space between the lines so that I may be able to alter your mistakes and correct them. These letters are too unequal, an ugly fault in writing. Notice how much greater *n* is than *e* and *o* than the circle you make of it. For the bodies of all the letters ought to be equal.

*Mend.* Tell us, pray, what do you mean by " bodies "?

## VIII. *Forming Letters in Writing*

*Teacher.* The middle part of the letters, the part besides the little heads and feet, if they have any; *b* and *l* have heads, *p* and *q* have feet. In this *m* the legs (or sides) are not equal in length. The first is shorter than the middle. It has also too long a tail, even as that *a* has. You don't sufficiently press the pen on the paper. The ink scarcely sticks, nor can you clearly distinguish what the beginnings of the letters are. Since you have tried to change these letters into others, having erased parts with the pointed end of your knife, you have disfigured your writing. It would have been better to draw a thin stroke through it. Then you should have transferred what remains of the word at the end of one line to the beginning of the next, only preserving the syllables always as wholes, for the law of Latin writing does not suffer them to be cut into. It is said that the Emperor Augustus did not have the custom of dividing words, nor did he transfer the overflowing letters of the end of his lines on to the next, but that he put them immediately under the line and round about it.

*Manr.* We will gladly imitate that, as it is the example of a king.

*Teacher.* You may well do so. For how could you otherwise satisfy yourselves that you had any connection with him (lit., that you are sprung from his blood)? But you must not join all the letters, nor must you separate all. There are those which must be ranged with one another, as those with tails, *e.g.*, *a*, *l*, *u*, together with others, and so the speared letters, *e.g.*, *f* and *t*. There are others which don't permit of this, viz., the circle-shaped *p*, *o*, *b*. As much as possible keep your head erect in writing, for if you bend and stoop, humours flow down on to the forehead and eyes, whence many diseases are born and whence too may come weakness of eyes. Now receive another copy and put it on paper for to-morrow, God willing (*Deo propitio*). As Ovid says (*Remedia Amoris*, 93):

Sed propera, nec te venturas differ in horas,
Qui non est hodie, cras minus aptus erit.[1]

and as Martial says (*de Notario*):

---

[1] But dispatch now, don't put off to future hours. Who does not do a thing to-day may be less able to do it to-morrow.

Currant verba licet, manus est velocior illis,
Nondum lingua suum, dextra peregit opus.[1]

*Mend.* Do you wish that we should imitate this blur?

*Teacher.* The blurs of correction certainly—and what
else is marked.

*Mend.* In the meantime we wish you the best of health.

---

[1] Let words run, the hand is quicker than they; not as yet has
the tongue done its work until the right hand has accomplished
its task.

# XI

## VESTITUS ET DEAMBULATIO MATUTINA—
*Getting Dressed and the Morning Constitutional*

BELLINUS, MALVENDA, JOANNIUS, GOMEZULUS

This dialogue (as its inscription indicates) has two divisions. The earlier part is a paraphrase of the first dialogue, for he treats of almost the same things as there, but more copiously: he describes the manner of putting on one's clothes or dressing one's self, and the kinds of clothes. The second part contains the morning constitutional, and includes a noteworthy description of spring as it reveals itself to all the senses.

### First Part

*Mal.*

> Nempe haec adsidue? Iam clarum mane fenestras intrat et angustas extendit lumine rimas: stertimus indomitum quod despumare Falernum sufficiat.[1]
> (*Persius*, iii. 1-3.)

*Bell.* It is plain to be seen that you are not in possession of your senses, for if you were, you would not be awake so long before morning, nor pour out verses, like a satyr's, by which you disclose your frenzy.

*Mal.* Then hear some epigrammatic verses, with no bite

---

[1] Is this always the order of the day, then? Here is full morning coming through the window-shutters, and making the narrow crevices look larger with the light; yet we go on snoring, enough to carry off the fumes of that unmanageable Falernian.— (Conington's Translation.)

80

in them and yet full of salt (*edentulos et salsos*).

Surgite iam pueris vendit ientacula pistor
Cristataeque sonant undique lucis aves.[1]

MARTIAL, 223.

*Bell.* The call of breakfast would drive off sleep from me more quickly than any din of thine.

*Mal.* Most happy jester, I wish you good morning.

*Bell.* And I wish you good night, and a good brain to be able to sleep as well as you speak with fluent oratory.

*Mal.* I beg you, answer me seriously, if you are ever able to answer seriously, what o'clock do you think it is now?

*Bell.* Midnight, or a little after.

*Mal.* By what clock?

*Bell.* That in my house.

*Mal.* Where is your house-clock? You would have to get or see a clock which had every hour for sleeping, eating, and playing, but which had none for studying.

*Bell.* Yet I have a clock by me.

*Mal.* Where? Produce it.

*Bell.* In my eyes. See, such as cannot be opened by any force. I beg of you, fall asleep again, or at least be quiet.

*Mal.* What in the name of evil is this drowsiness or, more truly, lethargy, and, in a certain sense, death? How long do you think we have slept?

---

[1] Arise, already the baker sells breakfast to boys. On every side, already, the birds announce the dawn by their chirping.

*Bell.* Two hours, or at the most three.

*Mal.* Three times three.

*Bell.* How is this possible?

*Mal.* Gomezulus, run along to the sun-dial of the Franciscans and see what hour it is.

*Bell.* Sun-dial, forsooth! When the sun has not as yet risen.

*Mal.* Risen, indeed! Come here, boy. Open that glass window that the sun with his beams may fall upon this fellow's eyes. Everything is full of the sun and the shadows are getting less.

*Bell.* What has the rising or setting of the sun to do with you? Let it rise earlier than you, since it has a longer day's journey to accomplish than you have.

*Mal.* Gomezulus, run quickly to St. Peter's, and there look both on the mechanical clock (*horologio machinali*), and on the style of the sun-dial to tell what time it is.

*Gom.* I have looked at both. By the sun-clock the shadow is yet a little distant from the second line. By the mechanical clock the hand points to a little after the hour of five.

*Bell.* What do you say? What else remains for you to do but fetch me the blacksmith from Stone Street, that he may separate my eye-lids by pincers so firmly stuck together? Tell him, that he has to force a door lever, from which the key has been lost.

*Gom.* Where does he live?

*Mal.* The boy will be going in earnest. Leave off joking and get up.

*Bell.* Well, let us get up, since you are so obstinate in mind. Ah! what a vexatious companion you are! Rouse me up, Christ, from the sleep of sin to the watchfulness of justice! Take me from the night of death into the light of life. Amen.

*Mal.* May this day proceed happily for you!

*Bell.* And for you, too, the same, and very many more as joyful and prosperous, *i.e.*, may you so pass through it that you neither harm the virtue of any one, nor may any one harm yours. Boy, bring me a clean shirt, for this one I have already worn for six whole days. There, snatch that flea on the leap. Now leave off the hunt. How small a matter it would be to have killed a single flea in this chamber!

*Mal.* As much as to take a drop of water out of the river Dilia (at Louvain).

*Bell.* Or yet from the ocean-sea itself. I won't have the shirt with the creased collar, but the other one with the smooth collar. For what are these creases otherwise at this time of the year than nests or receptacles for lice and fleas.

*Mal.* Stupid! You will then suddenly become rich, possessing both white and black stock.

*Bell.* Property abounding in quantity rather than of value in itself, and companions I would rather see in the neighbourhood than in my house! Order the maid to sew again the side of this shirt, and that with silk thread.

*Gom.* She hasn't any.

*Bell.* Then with flax or with wool, or even if she pleases

with hemp.  Never has this maid what is necessary; of what is unnecessary she has more than enough.  But you, Gomezulus, I don't want you to be a prophet.  Carry out my order and report to me.  Don't foretell what will happen.  Shake the dust out of the stockings and then clean them carefully with that hard fly-brush.  Give me clean socks, for these are now moist and smell of the feet. φεῦ, take them away, the smell annoys me terribly.

*Gom.*  Do you wish an under-garment?

*Bell.*  No, for by the light of the sun I gather that the day will be hot.  But reach me that velvet doublet with the half sleeves of silken cloth, and the light tunic of British cloth with long cloth cords.

*Mal.*  Or rather German cloth.  But what is the meaning of all this, whereby you think of making yourself so extraordinarily smart, beyond your custom—especially when it is not a feast-day?  And you ask also for country shoe-straps.

*Bell.*  And you?  Why have you put on your smooth silk, fresh from the tailor's, although you have your goat's-hair clothes and your well-worn clothes of Damascus.

*Mal.*  I have sent them to be repaired.

*Bell.*  I indeed rather consider ease in my clothes than ornament.  These little hooks and knobs are out of their place.  You always loosen them wrongly and thoughtlessly.

*Mal.* I rather use buttons and holes, which are more of an ornament, and less burdensome for putting on and taking off one's clothes.

*Bell.* Every one has not the same judgment on this any more than on other matters. Put down this breast-covering here in the box, and don't bring it out again during the whole of the summer. These straps have quite lost their strength. This belt is unsewn and torn to pieces. See that it is mended, but take care that no unshapely knots are sewn on.

*Gom.* This will not be done for at least an hour and a half.

*Bell.* Then stick a needle through it, so that it doesn't hang down. Give me the garters.

*Gom.* Here they are! I have got ready for you your shoes and the sandals with the long latchets. I have shaken off the dust from them well.

*Bell.* Rather wipe off the dirt from the shoes and polish them.

*Mal.* Is the *ligula* (shoe latchet) in the shoe? Concerning this word there has been a very sharp controversy amongst grammarians, as there usually is about everything, whether it should be called *ligula* or *lingula* (a little tongue).

*Bell.* The strap is sewn on the Spanish shoes over the top of the sole. Here they do not wear it so.

*Mal.* And in Spain they have given up arranging it so, because they now wear their shoes in the French fashion.

*Bell.* Let me have your ivory comb.

*Mal.* Where is your wooden one—the one from Paris?

*Bell.* Did you not hear me yesterday scolding Gomezulus?

*Mal.* Do you call beating a person scolding him?

*Bell.* This was the reason. He had broken five or six of the thick and of the thin teeth of the comb —almost broken them all to pieces.

*Mal.* I have lately read that a certain author stated that we should comb the head with an ivory comb forty times from the forehead to the top and then to the back of the head. What are you doing? That is not combing but stroking. Let me have the comb.

*Bell.* Nor is that combing, but shaving or sweeping. I think your head is made of bricks.

*Mal.* And I think yours is of butter—so that you dare not touch it closely.

*Bell.* Are you willing, then, that we should have a butting match with our heads?

*Mal.* I am not willing to have a senseless contest with you, nor to engage my good mind against your witless one. Now at length wash well your hands and face, but especially the mouth, that you may speak more clearly.

*Bell.* Would that I could cleanse my mind as quickly as my hands! Give me the wash-hand-basin.

*Mal.* Rub together more diligently the knuckles of your hands, to which there sticks the thickest dirt.

*Bell.* You are mistaken, for I think it is rather dis-coloured and wrinkled skin. Pour the water in these hand-basins, Gomezulus, into that sink and give me that net-bag and that striped cap. Bring now my boots (*ocreas*, lit. *greaves*).

*Gom.* Travelling boots?

*Bell.* No, my city boots.

*Gom.* Do you wish your Spanish cap and the long mantle?

*Bell.* Are we going out of doors?

*Mal.* Why not?

*Bell.* Bring then the travelling cloak.

*Mal.* Then at last we will go out, so as not to let slip by the time for having a walk.

## Second Part

*Bell.* Lead us, Christ, in the ways which are pleasing to Thee, in the name of the Father, the Son, and the Holy Spirit. Amen. Oh, how beautiful is the dawn! truly rosy and golden, as the poets call it. How I rejoice to have arisen. Let us go out of the city.

*Mal.* Yes, let us go. For I have not stepped foot out of the city gate for a whole week. But whither shall we first go, and after that which way shall we take?

*Bell.* To the citadel, or to the Carthusian Monastery?

*Mal.* Or to the meadows of St. James?

*Bell.* No, not there in the morning; rather in the evening.

*Mal.* To the Carthusian Monastery, then, past the Franciscan Monastery and the Recreation Grounds, thence through the Brussels gate, then we will return by the Carthusian Monastery to divine service. See, here is Joannius. A greeting to you, Joannius!

*Joan.* The warmest of greetings to you! What an

unusual thing is this that you should be stirring so early?

*Bell.* I was bound in the deepest sleep, but Malvenda here, by shouting and pinching me, tore me from my bed.

*Joan.* He did rightly, for this walk in the country will revive you and freshen you up. Let us go on the green walk (the *Pomerium*). O marvellous and adorable Creator of beauty so great; this world is not inappropriately called Mundus and by the Greeks Κόσμος, as if it were decked and made elegant with beauty.

*Mal.* Don't let us take our walk as if in a rush, but slowly and gently. Please let us make the circuit of the city walls twice or three times so that we may contemplate so splendid a view the more peacefully and freely.

*Description of Spring—1. Sight.   2. Hearing*

*Joan.* Observe, there is no sense which has not a lordly enjoyment! First, the eyes! What varied colours, what clothing of the earth and trees, what tapestry! What paintings are comparable with this view? Here are natural and real things; the representations are artificial and false. Not without truth has the Spanish poet, Juan de Mena, called May the painter of the Earth. Then, the ear. How delightful to hear the singing of birds, and especially the nightingale! Listen to her as she sings in the thicket, from whom, as Pliny says, issues the modulated sound of the completed science of music. Attend accurately and you will note all varieties of sounds. At one time there is no pause in them, but continuously, with breath held equably over a long time without change, the bird sings on. Now it changes tone! Now it sings in shorter and sharper tones! Now it draws in its tones and, as it were, makes its voice tremulous! Now it stretches out its voice and now it calls it back! At other times it sings long and, as it were, heroical verses; at other times, short sapphics, and at intervals very short, as in adonics. In very fact you have, as it were, the whole study and school of music in the nightingale. The little ones ponder and listen to the verses, which they imitate. The little bird listens with keen intentness (would that our teachers received like attention!) and gives back the sound. And then, again, they are silent.

### 3. *Smell.*   4. *Taste.*   5. *Touch*

The correction by example and a certain criticism from the teacher-bird are closely observed. But Nature leads them aright, whilst human beings exercise their will wrongly. Add to this there is a sweet scent breathing in from every side, from the meadows, from the crops, and from the trees, even from the fallow-land and neglected fields! Whatsoever you lift to your mouth has its relish, as even from the very air itself, like the earliest and softest honey.

*Mal.* This seems to me to be accounted for by what I have heard said by some, that in the month of May, bees are wont to gather their honey from celestial dew.

*Joan.* This was the opinion of many. If you wish anything to be offered to the touch, what softer or more healthful than the air we breathe on every side? For by its bracing breath it infuses itself through the veins and the whole body. Some verses of Vergil on spring come into my mind which I will hum to you, if you can listen to my voice, which I am afraid sounds more like that of a goose than of a swan—although, for my part, I would rather have a goose's voice than that of a swan, who only sings sweetly if he is just approaching his fate.

*Bell.* I, indeed, as far as I may answer on my own behalf, have a keen desire to hear the verses, with any voice you like, if only you will give us an explanation of the verses.

*Mal.* My opinion is not otherwise from that of Bellinus.
*Joan.*

Non alios prima crescentis origine mundi
Inluxisse dies, aliumve habuisse tenorem
Crediderim: ver illud erat: ver magnus agebat
Orbis, et hybernis parcebant flatibus Euri,
Quum primae lucem pecudes hausêre, virumque
Terrea progenies duris caput extulit arvis,
Immissaeque ferae sylvis et sidera caelo.
Nec res hunc tenerae possent perferre laborem

Si non tanta quies iret frigusque caloremque
Inter, et exciperet caeli indulgentia terras.[1]

*Georgics*, ii. 336-345.

*Bell.* I have not quite followed it.

*Mal.* And I still less, as I think.

*Joan.* Learn the verses thoroughly, or you won't understand them, for they are taken from the depths
of philosophy, as are very many others of that
poet.

*Mal.* We will question the schoolmaster Orbilius
about them, for here he is coming to meet us.

## The Mind

*Joan.* He is by no means the man to meet the difficulty.
Let us just salute him and let him go his
way, for he is a fierce man, fond of flogging
(*plagosus*), imbued with a vast haughtiness,
instead of being learned in literature, although
he has seriously persuaded himself that he is
the Alpha of learned teachers. Moreover, we
have only spoken of the body. How greatly
are the soul and mind exhilarated and aroused
by such an early morning as this! There is

[1] " Such days, I trow, at the infancy of earth,
Shone forth, and kept the tenor of their birth;
True spring was that, the world was bent on spring,
And eastern breezes check'd their wintry wing:
While cattle drank new light, and man was shown,
A race of iron from a land of stone;
Then savage beasts were launch'd upon the grove,
And constellations on the heaven above;
Nor could young Nature have achieved the birth,
Unless a period of repose so sweet
Had come to pass, betwixt the cold and heat,
And heaven's indulgence greeted the new earth."

R. D. Blackmore's Translation.

no time so suitable for good learning, for
observing things, and for attentively listening
to what is said, and whatever you read; nor
is it otherwise with reflection and with thinking a problem out, whatever it may be. You
can give your mind to it. Not undeservedly
has it been said: "The dawn (*Aurora*) is most
pleasing to the Muses."

*Bell.* But let me tell you I'm famishing with hunger.
Let us get back home to breakfast.

*Mal.* What then will you have?

*Bell.* Bread, butter, cherries, waxen-coloured prunes,
which so greatly seem to have pleased our
Spaniards that they call all plums by this
name.[1] Or should they not have such food at
home, we will pluck some leaves of the oxtongue (*buglossa*), and we will add some sage
in place of butter.

*Mal.* Shall we have wine to drink?

*Bell.* By no means—but beer, and that of the weakest,
of yellow Lyons, or else pure and liquid water,
drawn from the Latin or Greek well.

*Mal.* Which do you call the Latin well and the Greek
well?

*Bell.* Vives is accustomed to call the well close to the
gate the Greek well; that one farther off he
calls the Latin well. He will give you his
reasons for the names when you meet him.

[1] As did Columella, *i.e.*, *pruna cereola*. Pliny calls them *cerina*.

# XII

## DOMUS—*The New House*

JOCUNDUS, LEO, VITRUVIUS

In this dialogue Vives describes the whole house and its parts, one by one, through the logical form of distribution of the whole into its parts. Concerning the details, *see* the books of Vitruvius on architecture, and Grapaldus.

The interlocutors were distinguished architects. Vitruvius is an author of antiquity; the other two are more recent. The one, Johannes Jocundus Veronensis, wrote, amongst other monuments of a not inelegant mind, a work on the *Commentaries of Julius Caesar*. The other, Baptista Albertus Leo, distinguished himself in an equally great degree.

*Joc.* Have you any knowledge of the occupier of this spacious and elegant house?

*Leo.* Most certainly; for he is a relation of the manservant of my father.

*Joc.* We will ask him to open the whole house to us, for they say that nothing could be more pleasant and delightful.

*Leo.* Let us go to it, and ring the little bell at the door, so as not to burst in unexpected. (Tat-tat.)

*Vitruvius Insularius.*[1] Who is there?

*Leo.* It is I.

*Vitr.* Hail! most welcome, sweetest boy! What brings you here now?

*Leo.* I come from school.

[1] Freigius's note: *Insularius* is equivalent to French *concierge*.

*Vitr.* But for what reason are you here?

*Leo.* My friend here and I would very much like to see over your house.

*Vitr.* Why, haven't you seen it before now?

*Leo.* No, not all of it.

### The Vestibulum—The Door—The Threshold

*Vitr.* Come in. Eh! boy, bring me the key for the doors of the house. First, this is the entrance-hall (*vestibulum*). It stands open the whole day, without guard, for it is not within the house, yet also it is not outside, though it is closed at night. Observe the magnificent door, the leaves of which are of oak and fitted with brass, and both the foot-piece and head-piece of the doorway are made of alabaster marble. In former times Hercules was set up at the door of the house to ward off mischief (ἀλεξίκακος). But here we place Christ, the true God, for Hercules was but a cruel and evil man. With Christ as guard no evil will enter into the house.

*Joc.* Οὐδὲ οὖν δεσπότης αὐτός (so not even its master).

*Vitr.* What is that he said in Greek?

*Joc.* Why should so many evil persons enter in?

*Vitr.* Well, if evil persons do get in, they can then bring nothing evil in with them.

*Leo.* Don't you have any door-angels?

*Vitr.* The custom has gone out in some nations.

### The Door—The Hall

Next comes the door of the entrance hall, which the hall servant (*atriensis servus*) answers.

He is the chief of the servants, as the house-
boy (*mediastinus*) is the least in position. Then
comes the spacious hall for walking in, and in it
are numerous and varied pictures.

*Joc.* Please, what are they all about?

*Vitr.* That is a representation of the foundations of
the heavens (*coeli facies ichnographica*). That
shows the plan of the earth and sea. There
you have the world newly discovered by
Spanish navigations. In that picture you see
Lucretia as she is killing herself.[1]

*Joc.* Please, what is she saying, for even as she is dying
she seems to say something?

*Vitr.* " Many are astounded at my deed because it is not
every one who has suffered such a grief."

*Joc.* I understand what she says.

*Leo.* What is the meaning of this picture delineated
with such varied figures?

*Vitr.* It is a sketch of this house. Draw back the covering from that picture. There!

*Joc.* What does it represent? A little old man who is
sucking his wife's breast?

## The Staircase

*Vitr.* Hast thou not read of this subject in the chapter
on Piety in Valerius Maximus.[2]

*Joc.* What does she say?

*Vitr.* " I do not yet pay back as much as I have
received."

*Joc.* What does the old man say?

[1] Livy, book i.
[2] Book v. cap. 4, de Cimone; Ovid, *Fasti*, book ii.

*Winding Stairs—The Floor—The Upper Story*

*Vitr.* " I rejoice that I have been born." Let us step up these winding-stairs.  The steps one by one, as you see, are broad and were made of whole pieces of basalt-marble.  This first story is the dwelling of the master, the upper story is for guests; not as if my master had a garret on lease far away, but there it is furnished for his guest friends always in order and free, unless filled already with guests.  This is the dining-room.

*The Dining-Room—The Window*

*Joc.* Good Christ! what transparent window panes these are and how artistically painted they are in shaded outlines!  What colours!  How life-like!  What pictures, what statues, what wainscoting!  What is the story pourtrayed on the panes?

*Vitr.* The fall of Griselda, which John Boccaccio wrote so aptly and skilfully; but my master has decided to add a true story to this fiction, which excels the story of Griselda, viz., that of Godelina of Flanders and the English Queen Catharine of Aragon.  The first of the statues is the Apostle Paul.

*Joc.* What is the inscription of the sculpture?

*Vitr.* " How much we owe thee, O Christ."

*Joc.* What does he say himself?

*Vitr.* " By the grace of God I am what I am and His

grace which was bestowed on me, was not in
vain." The other statue is Mutius Scaevola.

*Joc.* But he is not mute even if he is called Mutius.
What is the inscription on his statue?

*Vitr.* " This fire will not burn me up because another
greater one burns in me." The third statue
is Helen; the writing states: " Oh, would that
I always had been such a statue, then should I
have wrought less harm."

*Joc.* What is the meaning of the old blind bald-headed
man who points his finger at Helen?

*Vitr.* That is Homer, who says to Helen: " Thy ill
deed has been well sung by me."

*Joc.* Look, the wainscoting is gilded, and here and there
decked with pearls.

*Vitr.* There are all kinds of pearls, but of small worth.

*Joc.* What do we look on from the windows?

### *The Summer-house—The Sleeping-room*

*Vitr.* These windows look into the gardens, those into the
court. This is the summer-house or garden
dining-room. Here you see a sleeping-room or
chamber. The sleeping-room is furnished with
tapestry, with a pavement wainscoted and
covered with rush-mats. There are some
pictures of the Holy Virgin, of Christ the
Saviour, and there are others of Narcissus,
Euryalus, Adonis, Polyxena, who are said to
have been of the highest beauty.

*Joc.* What is written on the upper lintel of the door?

*Vitr.* " Withdraw from your troubles and enter the
haven of peace."

*Joc.* What is written inside the door-post?

*Vitr.* " Bring into this haven no tempest." The most necessary house utensils are kept in that closed chamber. The other is the winter chamber. As you see, everything there is darker and better covered. Then there is a sweating chamber.

### The Sweating Chamber

*Joc.* It is bigger in my opinion than the dining-room would lead one to expect.

*Vitr.* Don't you notice that the inner sleeping-room is heated by the same steam-pipe?

*Joc.* They say that if sleeping-rooms had no chimney flue they would be warmer.

*Vitr.* It is not usual to have them in the air-holes.

*Joc.* What is that room, so elegantly vaulted?

### The Chapel

*Vitr.* It is the chapel (*lararium*) or sanctuary (*sacellum*) in which divine service (*res divina*) is held.

*Joc.* Where is the *latrina* ?

*Vitr.* We have it up in the granary out of the way. In the sleeping-rooms my master uses basins, pans, and chamber-crockery.

*Joc.* How beautifully and artistically made are all these little towers and pyramids and columns and weathercocks!

### The Kitchen—Eating Chamber—The Cellar

*Vitr.* We will now go down. This is the kitchen; this

the eating-chamber; here is the wine-cellar
and the larder, where we are annoyed by the
attempts of thieves to get in.

*Joc.* How can thieves get in here? It is, as it seems to
me, so carefully closed in, and the windows
have iron gratings?

*Vitr.* Through chinks and borings.

*Leo.* There are also mice and weasels who strip you of
all kinds of food!

## The Back-door

*Vitr.* This is the back-door of the house, which, when
the master is not at home, is always fastened
with two bars, both locked and bolted.

*Leo.* Why have these windows no iron bars?

*Vitr.* Because they are only rarely open and they abut,
as you see, on a narrow and dark by-street.
Rarely any one puts his head out of the
window. Therefore my master has decided
that he will have them latticed.

*Leo.* With what kind of bars?

*Vitr.* Perhaps with wooden bars. It is not yet certain.
In the meantime this fastening suffices.

## The Portico

*Joc.* What high columns and a portico full of majesty!
See how these Atlantides and Caryatides seem
to strive to support the building against falling,
whilst really they are doing nothing.

*Leo.* There are many people like them, who appear to
accomplish great things when they are in

reality leading leisurely and sluggish lives; drones who enjoy the fruits of the labours of others. But what is that house there below, adjoining this, but badly built and full of cracks?

*Vitr.* It is the old house. Because it had cracks and had great lack of repair, my master decided to have this new one built, from the foundation. That old one is now a resting-place for birds and the habitation of rats, but we shall soon take it down.

# XIII

## SCHOLA—*The School*

Tyro, Spudaeus

In this dialogue the school is described in six parts, as teachers, honours, hours of learning and repetition, books, library, the disputation. The name *Tyro* is that of the crude novice, a metaphor taken from military affairs of those as yet unskilled in war, to whom are opposed the *veterani*. *Spudaeus* is in Greek the diligent and industrious person, a name worthy of one who is studious.

## I. *The Teachers*

*Tyro.* What a delightful and magnificent school! I suppose there is not in the whole academy any part more excellent.

*Spud.* You judge rightly; add, also, what is of more importance, that elsewhere there are no more cultured and prudent teachers, who with such dexterity pass on their learning.

*Tyro.* It behoves us then to repay their trouble by attaining great knowledge.

*Spud.* And this indeed by great shortening of the labour of learning!

*Tyro.* What does the schooling cost?

*Spud.* You can at once give up so base and unreasonable a question. Can one in a matter of so great moment inquire as to payment? The very teachers themselves do not bargain for reward, nor is it suitable for their pupils to even think about it.   For what reward could be adequate?   Have you never heard the declaration of Aristotle that gods, parents, and masters can never be sufficiently recompensed?   God created the whole man, the parents gave the body birth, the masters form the mind.

*Tyro.*  What do those masters teach, and for how long?

*Spud.*  Each one has his separate class-room and the masters are for various subjects.   Some impart with labour and drudgery the whole day long the elements of the art of grammar; others take more advanced work in the same subject; others propound rhetoric, dialectic, and the remaining branches of knowledge, which are called liberal or noble arts.

*Tyro.*  Why are they so-called?

*Spud.*  Because every noble-minded person must be instructed in them.   They are in contrast to the illiberal subjects of the market-place which are practised by the labour of the body or hands, which pertain to slaves and men who have but little wit.   Amongst scholars some are " tyrones " and others " batalarii."

II. *Grades or Honours of Scholars—Tyro—Baccalaureus —Licentiates—Doctors*

*Tyro.*  What do these names signify?

*Spud.*  Both these names are taken from the art of warfare.   " Tyro " is an old word used with regard to the one who is beginning the practice of war. " Batalarius " is the French name of the soldier who has already once been in a fight (which they call a battle) and has engaged in a close fight and has raised his hand against the foe, and so in the literary contests at Paris, " batalarius " has begun to signify the man who has disputed publicly in any art. Teachers are chosen from them, and are called " licentiates," because it is permitted them to teach, or, better still, they might be termed " designate," *i.e.*, the men marked out. At least they have taken the doctorate. Before the whole university, a hat is placed on their head as a sign that they have had their freedom conferred on them, and become *emeriti*. This is the supreme honour and the highest grade of dignity. .

*Tyro.* Who is that with so great a company round him, before whom march staff-bearers with silver staffs?

### The Rector

*Spud.* That is the Principal (*Rector*) of the Academy. Many are drawn to him because of the honour they bear him in his office.

*Tyro.* How often in the day are the boys taught?

### III. *Hours of Teaching and Repetition*

*Spud.* Several times. One hour before sunrise; two hours in the morning; two hours in the afternoon.

*Tyro.* So often?

*Spud.* An old custom of the Academy so establishes it. And in addition the scholars repeat and think over what they have received in instruction from their masters, like as if they were chewing the cud of their lessons.

*Tyro.* With so much noise over it?

*Spud.* Such is now their practice!

*Tyro.* To what purpose?

*Spud.* So as to learn.

*Tyro.* On the contrary, so as to shout. For they don't seem to meditate on their studies, but to be preparing themselves for the office of public crier. That one there is clearly raving. For if he had a sound brain, he would neither so call out, nor gesticulate, nor so distort himself.

*Spud.* They are Spaniards and Frenchmen, somewhat impetuous, and as they hold divers opinions, they contend the more warmly as if for their hearths and altars, as it is said.

*Tyro.* What! are the teachers here of different opinions?

*Spud.* Sometimes they teach contradictory views.

*Tyro.* What authors are they interpreting?

### IV. *Authors*

*Spud.* Not all the same, but each one as he is furnished with skill and knowledge. The most erudite teachers take to themselves the best authors with the sharpest judgment, those whom you grammarians call classics. There are those who, on account of their ignorance of what is better, descend to the lowest (*ad proletarios*) and are worthy of condemnation.

## V. *The Library*

Let us enter. I will show you the public library of this school. It looks, according to the precept of great men, to the east.

*Tyro.* Wonderful! How many books, how many good authors, Greek and Latin orators, poets, historians, philosophers, theologians, and the busts of authors!

*Spud.* And indeed, as far as could be done, delineated to the life and so much the more valuable! All the book-cases and book-shelves are of oak or cypress and with their own little chains. The books themselves for the most part are bound in parchment and adorned with various colours.

*Tyro.* What is that first one with rustic face and nose turned-up?

*Spud.* Read the inscription.

*Tyro.* It is Socrates and he says: "Why do I appear in this library when I have written nothing?"

*Spud.* Those who follow him, Plato and Xenophon, answer: "Because thou hast said what others wrote." It would take long to go through the things here, one by one.

*Tyro.* Pray what are those books thrown on a great heap there?

*Spud. The Catholicon,* Alexander, Hugutio, Papias, disputations in dialectics, and books of sophistries in physics. These are the books which I called "worthy of condemnation."

*Tyro.* Nay rather, they are condemned to violent death!

*Spud.* They are all thrown out.  Let him take them
who will;  he will free us of a troublesome
burden.

*Tyro.* Oh, how many asses would be necessary for carrying them away!  I am astonished that they
have not been taken away, when there is so
great an assembly of asses everywhere.  Some-
where in that heap the books of Bartolus and
Baldus are lying together and others of that
quality (*hujus farinae*).

*Spud.* Say rather of that coarseness (*furfuris*).  The
loss would not be hurtful to the tranquillity of
mankind.

*Tyro.* Look, who are those with those flowing hoods?


VI. *The Disputation—*1. *The Praeses.*

*Spud.* Let us go down.  They are " batalarii," going to
the disputation.

*Tyro.* Please lead us thither.

*Spud.* Step in, but quietly and reverently.  Uncover
your head and watch attentively all, one by
one, for there is a discussion beginning on
weighty matters which will conduce greatly to
one's knowledge.  That one whom you see
sitting alone in the highest seat is the president
(*praeses*) of the disputation and the judge of
the disputes, so to say, the Agonotheta.  His
first duty is to appoint the place for each of
the contenders, lest there should be any dis-
order or confusion, if one or other should want
to take precedence.

# Schola

*Tyro.* What is the meaning of the skin-covering of his toga?

*Spud.* It is his doctor's robe, the emblem of his position and dignity. He is a man of whom there are few so learned, who, by the choice of the candidates in theology, carried off the first prize, and by the most learned of the faculty is regarded as the first among them.

*Tyro.* They say that Bardus was the first choice in his year.

*Spud.* He beat all his competitors by canvassing and craft, not by his knowledge.

*Tyro.* Who is that thin and pallid man they all rush upon?

2. *The Propugnator.* 3. *The Oppugnator (a smart man) —The Vapid Man—The Smooth Man.*

*Spud.* He is the *propugnator*, who will receive the attack of all, and who has become thin and pale by his immoderate night-watches. He has done great things in philosophy and is advanced in theology. But now you must be quiet and listen, for he who is now making the attack is accustomed to think out his arguments most acutely and subtly, and presses most keenly the *propugnator*, and, in the opinion of all, is compared with the very highest in this discipline, and often compels his antagonist to recant. Notice how the latter has tried to elude him, but how the *oppugnator* has met him effectively by his irrefutable reasoning,

and how the *propugnator* cannot escape him!
This arrow cannot be avoided. His argument
is like an invincible Achilles. It enters the
neck of the opponent. The *propugnator* cannot
protect himself and soon will give in (*manus
dabit*) unless some god suggests a subterfuge
to his mind. Behold, the question is brought
to an end by the decision of the judge
(*decretor*). Now I loosen your tongue to speak
as you wish. For he who now attacks is as
vapid wine, and contends as with a leaden
dagger, yet he shouts louder than the rest.
Notice, and you will see that he grows hoarse
from the encounter. Though his weapons are
repulsed, he presses on none the less pertina-
ciously, but without effect; nor does any one
wish to have the reversion to his argument, or
to have him assuaged by the answer of the
defender or the president. He who now
enters the contest effeminately begs the judge
for his permission, and speaks with courtesy,
though he argues ineffectively and always
leaves off tired, even gasping, as if he had gone
through the unpleasant business with fortitude.
Let us depart.

# XIV

## CUBICULUM ET LUCUBRATIO—*The Sleeping-room and Studies by Night*

PLINIUS, EPICTETUS, CELSUS, DYDIMUS

In this dialogue Vives treats of two matters: in the first place
he describes night-studies with adjuncts of time, causes, and
subjects; then the bed, its apparatus and adjuncts. The assist-
ing causes (*causae adjuvantes*) of night-study are lights, the
night-study gown, Minerva or Christ, table, bookcase, reader
(*anagnostes*), a scribe (*exceptor*), pens, sand-case (*theca pulveraria*).
The subjects are Cicero, Demosthenes, Nazianzenus, Xenophon.
The apparatus of the bed consists in a mattress, a bolster,
cushions, sheets, coverlets, curtains, mosquito-curtain, hangings,
rugs. Adjuncts are—gnats, fleas, lice, bugs, a striking clock, a
folding seat, a pot, a lyre. The names of the persons are aptly
allotted, for they were the four most learned and studious men,
concerning whom Volaterranus has written in his *Anthropologia*.
Plinius wrote *De Historia Naturali*, in xxxvii. books. He was the
uncle of the other Pliny whose letters are still extant. The
latter writes thus to Marcus, of his uncle: " He was sharp-
witted, of incredible studiousness, of the highest vigilance, most
sparing of sleep. After food (which he used to take in the day-
time, of a light and easily digestible kind, according to the
custom of the ancients), if he had leisure, often in the
summer, he would lie in the sun. Then read his book, anno-
tate it, and make extracts. He never read without making
extracts. He was even accustomed to say that no book was so
bad as not to be profitable in some part of it. I remember once
when a reader had pronounced something wrongly, one of his
friends had the man called up and made him repeat it, whereupon my uncle said: ' You understood, forsooth? ' He nodded.
' Then why have the passage recalled? We have lost more than
ten verses by this interruption.' So great was his economy of
time. This, too, in the midst of his labours in the noise of the
town. Even in the retirement of his bath he spent his time in
studies. When I say the bath, I speak of the inner parts of the
house generally. For whilst he was stretching himself or drying

109

himself, he used to listen to reading or to dictate. On a journey, as if relieved from other cares, he occupied himself in study only. At his side was an amanuensis with a book and writing tablets, whose hands were furnished in winter with gloves, so that by no roughness of weather should any time be snatched from studies. For the same reason, when at Rome, he was carried about in a chair. I recall that I was reproved by him when I went for a walk. ' Are you not able,' said he, ' not to waste your time?' For he thought all time wasted which was not devoted to studies." For an account of his death, see an epistle by the same writer to Tacitus.

Epictetus (as the epigram concerning him testifies) was both a slave and lame. He was poorer than Irus.[1] But in wisdom and equanimity of mind and constancy (as records about him testify) he was admirable and almost divine. But he was the servant of Epaphroditus the freedman of the Emperor Nero. Celsus was a renowned physician, whose works are still extant, whose excellent *dictum* was: "That many grave diseases are cured by abstinence and quiet."

Dydimus, the grammarian, on account of the almost incredible number of books which he is said to have written, is called χαλκέντερος, as if having intestines of brass, *i.e.*, he was remarkably patient and indefatigable in labour. He (as also Origen) was called Adamantinus. On this same matter *see* Proverb: Adamantinus and Chalcenterus and the lamp of Aristophanes and Cleanthes.

## I. *Studies by Night*

*Plin.* It is five o'clock in the afternoon. Epictetus, shut me the window and bring me light. I will work with a light.

*Epict.* What light do you wish?

*Plin.* For the time being, whilst others are present, tallow or wax candles; when they have retired, take them away and place here for me the lampstand.

*Cels.* What for?

*Plin.* For working.

[1] *I.e.*, the beggar in the house of Ulysses at Ithaca. See Martial, 5, 41, 9.

*Time*

*Cels.* Don't you study better in the morning? Then it seems to me the season of the time and the condition of the body invite study, since at that time there is the least exhalation from the brain, digestion having been completed.

*Plin.* But this hour is very quiet, when every one has gone to rest and everything is silent, and for those who eat at mid-day and morning it is not inconvenient. Some follow the old custom and only eat one meal and that in the evening; others merely at mid-day, according to the advice of the new doctors; and again others both mid-day and evening, according to the usage of the Goths.

*Cels.* But were there no mid-day meals before the Goths?

*Plin.* There were, but light meals. The Goths introduced the custom of eating to satiety twice a day.

*Cels.* On that account Plato condemned the meal-times of the Syracusans, who had two good meals every day.

*Circumstances Aiding Studies*

*Plin.* For that very reason you may conclude that people like the Syracusans were very rare.

*Cels.* Enough of them! Why do you prefer to work with a lamp than a candle?

*Plin.* On account of the equable flame, which less tries

the eyes, for the flicker of the wick injures the eyes and the odour of the tallow is unpleasant.

*Cels.* Then use wax candles, the odour of which is not displeasing.

*Plin.* In them the wick is more flickering and the vapour is no more healthy. In the tallow lights the wick is for the most part of linen and not of cotton, as the tradesmen seek to make a profit on all these things by fraud. Pour oil into this lamp, bring a candle and take out the wick and clean it.

*Epict.* Notice how the lampblack sticks to the needle. They say this is a sign of rain, in the same manner as we find in Vergil:—

Scintillare oleum et putres concrescere fungos.[1]

*Plin.* Bring hither also the snuffers and clean this candle. But don't throw the black on the floor lest it smoke, but press it into the snuffers-box whilst it is held together. Bring me my dressing-gown, that long one lined with skin.

*Cels.* I will provide you with your books. May Minerva be favourable to you!

*Plin.* May Paul or, what I should rather have said, may Jesus Christ, the Wisdom of God, be with me.

*Cels.* Perhaps Christ is adumbrated in the fable of Minerva and that of the birth from Jupiter's brain.

---

[1] *Georgics*, i. 392.   The oil (of lamps is seen) to sparkle and crumbling fungus to form.

*Plin.* Place the table on the supports in the sleeping-chamber.

*Cels.* Do you prefer the table to the desk?

*Plin.* At this time, yes; but place a small desk on the table.

*Epict.* A self-standing one or a movable one?

*Plin.* Which you like. But where is the Dydimus of my studies?

*Cels.* I will summon him thither.

### Subjects of Study

*Plin.* Fetch also my boy-scribe. For I should like to dictate something. Give me those reed-pens and two or three feather pens, those with thick stalk, and the sand-case. Bring me also from the chest the Cicero and Demosthenes, and from the desk, the book in which I make all my notes and important extracts. Do you hear? And my extemporaneous MS. book in which I will polish up some passages.

*Dyd.* I believe the MS. book is not in the desk but in the chest, locked up.

*Plin.* Do you yourself search for it. And bring me the Nazianzenus.

*Dyd.* I don't know it.

*Plin.* The book is of slight thickness, sewn together and roughly bound in parchment. Bring also the volume, the fifth from the end.

*Dyd.* What is its title?

*Plin.* Xenophon's *Commentaries*. The book is in finished style. It is bound in leather with fastenings and knobs of copper.

*Dyd.* I don't find it.

*Plin.* Now I remember. I put it in the fourth case.
Fetch it. In the same case there are only
loose sheets and rough books just as they have
come straight from the press.

*Dyd.* Which volume of Cicero do you want, for there are
four?

*Plin.* The second.

*Epict.* It is not yet back from the book-gluer, who had
it, I believe, five days ago to glue.

*Dyd.* How do you like that pen?

*Plin.* On that point I am not very particular; whatever comes into my hand I use it as if it were
good.

*Dyd.* You have learned that from Cicero.

*Plin.* You just be quiet. Open me the Cicero. Look
me up three or four pages of the *Tusculan
Questions.* Seek the passages on gentleness
and joy.

*Epict.* Whose verses are these?

*Plin.* They are his own translations of Sophocles. This
he does with keen pleasure and therefore often.

*Epict.* He was, I think, sufficiently apt in writing verses.

*Dyd.* Most apt and facile, and, for his time, not unhappy
in his verse, contrary to what very many think.

*Epict.* But wherefore hast thou left off pursuing the art
of poetry?

## II. *The Bed—Its Equipment*

*Plin.* I hope that we yet at times may take it up again
in leisure hours, for there is much alleviation
in it from more serious studies. I am already

weary of studies, meditation, writing.   Stretch
out my bed.

*Epict.* In which sleeping-room?

*Plin.* In the big square room.   Take away the reclining
cushion out of the corner, and put it in
the dining-room.   Place over the feather-bed
another of wool.   See also that the supports of
the bed are sufficiently firm.

*Epict.* What is it that is troubling you?   For you don't
lie on one part or other of the frame-work, but
in the middle of the bed.   It would be more
healthy for you if the bed were harder and one
which would offer resistance to your body.

*Plin.* Take the head-pillow away, and instead of it put
two cushions, and in this heat I prefer that
lightly woven, to the linen, cloth.

*Epict.* Without bed-covering!

*Plin.* Yes.

*Epict.* You will get cold, for the body is exhausted by
studies.

*Plin.* Then put on a light covering.

*Epict.* These?   And no more?

*Plin.* No.   If I feel cold in bed, then I will ask for more
clothes.   Take away the curtains, for I prefer
a mosquito-net for the keeping off of gnats, a
net of fine gauze (*conopeum*).

*Epict.* I have noticed but few gnats, though of fleas and
lice a pretty fair number.

### Adjuncts

*Plin.* I am surprised that you notice anything particularly, for you sleep and snore so soundly.

*Epict.* No one sleeps better than he who does not feel
how badly he is sleeping.

*Plin.* None of the insects with which we are troubled in
bed in summer disgust me so much as the
bugs because of their ghastly odour.

*Epict.* Of which there is a good supply in Paris and
Lyons.

*Plin.* At Paris there is a kind of wood which produces them, and in Lyons the potter's earth.
Place my alarum-clock here, and place the
pointer for four o'clock in the morning, for I
don't wish to sleep later. Take my shoes off,
and place here the folding-chair in which I
may sit. Let the chamber-crockery be set
near the bed on a foot-stool. I don't know
what it is that causes a bad smell here. Fumi-
gate with frankincense or juniper. Sing to
me something on the lyre as I go to bed after
the custom of Pythagoras, so that I may the
more quickly fall asleep, and my dreams may
be the more peaceful.

*Epict.*

Somne, quies rerum, placidissime, somne, deorum,
Pax animi, quem cura fugit, qui corpora duris
Fessa ministeriis mulces, reparasque labori.[1]

OVID, *Metamorph.* book xi. ll. 623-5.

---

[1] Sleep, the rest of things, sleep, most gracious of the gods,
peace of the mind, whom anxiety shuns, thou who soothest the
weary bodies from their hard duties and restorest them for their
labour.

# XV

## CULINA—*The Kitchen*

### LUCULLUS, APICIUS, PISTILLARIUS, ABLIGURINUS

In this dialogue Vives describes the matters which concern the kitchen. Nor is it any disgrace for a noble youth to be able to call things, one by one, by their right names, as also the interpreter of Aristophanes thinks in the *Acharnians* :—

ἔστι δὲ τοῦτο ἀστεῖον καὶ πεπαιδευμένῳ ἁρμόξον, μήδε τῶν κατὰ τὴν οἰκίαν σκευ ῶν τῆς καθημερινῆς χρείας, ἀγνοεῖν τὰ ὀνόματα.[1]

The names of the interlocutors are aptly chosen, as is always the case. Lucullus and Apicius are fit names of men noted for luxury. As to Lucullus, see Plutarch in his *Lucullus and Athenaeus*, book xii., who says that he:—

τρυφῆς πρῶτον εἰς ἄπαν Ῥωμαίοις ἡγεμόνα γενέσθαι.[2]

Also in Book iv. he says:—

τὸν Ἀπίκιον περὶ ἀσωτίᾳ πάντας ἀνθρώπους ὑπερηκοντικέναι.[3]

Pistillarius and Abligurinus are fictitious names; the former from the pounder of a mortar, and as if the epithet for an obtuse man; the latter from a " licking away," as of a gourmand. This dialogue may be divided into three parts, the management of the kitchen by Apicius, his precepts, and songs.

## I. *The Hiring of Apicius*

*Luc.* Are you an eating-house keeper (*popino*) ?

*Apic.* I am.

---

[1] This is a mark of refinement and seemly in one who is cultured —not to be ignorant of the names of the utensils that are in daily use in the house.

[2] *Athen.* 12. That he was the first to set the Romans the example of luxury in all things.

[3] That Apicius exceeded all men in prodigality.

*Luc.* Where do you work?

*Apic.* At the eating-house called the Poultry-Cock (*galli gallinacei*). Do you want my services?

*Luc.* Yes, for a wedding.

*Apic.* Let me then hasten home, so that I may give instructions to my wife how to treat the gourmandisers (whom I know are not wont to be lacking in this city) and their guests who are invited.

*Luc.* Do you hear? You will find me in the Stone Street—in the shoemakers' district.

*Apic.* I will soon be with you.

*Luc.* Very well. Get to your cook-shop.

## II. *The Precepts of Apicius*

*Apic.* Hallo! Pistillarius and Abligurinus, make a fire with big logs on the hearth under the flue, and let them be as dry as possible.

*Pist.* Do you think you are at Rome? Here we have not stalls for the sale of dry wood from which dry logs can be got. But this which I have will be dry enough.

*Apic.* If you don't get it dry enough, Abligurinus, you will, by your work of blowing up the flame, lose your eyesight.

*Ablig.* Then I shall drink so much the more freely. Curse the wine!

*Apic.* Curse the water! For you shall not touch wine to-day if I keep in my right mind. I am not going to let you overturn the vessels, and break the small pots to pieces, and ruin the food.

*Ablig.* This fire won't burn!

*Apic.* Throw in a small bundle of sticks smeared in brimstone, and kindling-wood, together with some chips.

*Ablig.* It is quite gone out.

*Apic.* Run across to the next house with the shovel and bring us a great big firebrand and some good live coal.

*Ablig.* The master of that house is a metal-worker, nor does he let a single piece of coal be taken from his furnaces but he has his eye on it (*citius oculum*).

*Apic.* He is not a metal-worker, but a metal-cutter; go therefore to the oven. What are you bringing there? This is not a firebrand; it is rather a torch (*titionem magis quam torrem*).

*Ablig.* They have not got burning coal.

*Apic.* What bad coal! You should rather call it turf. Move these logs and stir the kindling wood with this poker so that it may gather flame. Use the *pyrolabum* (the tongs), you ass!

*Ablig.* What thing does that word signify?

*Apic.* *Forceps ignaria* (tongs for the fire), a *pruniceps* (a fire-stirrer).

*Ablig.* Why do you give me words in Greek, as if there were not Latin words for the things?

*Apic.* Are asses also grammarians?

*Ablig.* What wonder, since grammarians are certainly *asses*.

*Apic.* Make an end of wrangling. I want some coals or pieces of turf lighting for me on this hearth, for cooking the cakes baked in earthen cups.

Hang the bronze vessel over the fire so that we can have plenty of hot water. Then throw into the cooking-pot that shoulder of mutton with the salted beef; add calf and lamb flesh, and stir the cooking vessel on the fire. In the *chytropus* [1] we will thoroughly boil the rice.

*Ablig.* What shall we do with the chickens?

*Apic.* They shall be cooked in brazen pots which are lined with tin, so that they may have a more pleasant taste. But don't bring them too soon; the meat-spits and the pans should be forthcoming about nine o'clock. Let this pike play about in the water a little, then skin him.

*Ablig.* Are there to be meat and fish at the same meal?

*Apic.* Decidedly, according to the German fashion.

*Ablig.* And is this approved by the doctors?

*Apic.* It is not in accordance with the art of medicine, but it will please the doctors. I thought this block of a man (*stips*) was merely a grammarian; he is also a doctor.

*Ablig.* Have you never heard of that question: Whether there are in a city more doctors or fools?

*Apic.* Who has thrust you into the kitchen, when you are such a salted herring (*saperda*)?

*Ablig.* My adverse fate.

*Apic.* Nay, what is quite clear,—it is thy sluggishness, carelessness, voracity, thy throat and thy stomach, thy degenerate and debased soul. Therefore must thou now run about with

[1] Cooking vessel with feet for coals.

naked feet, half-clothed, in old torn garments
which don't cover you behind.

*Ablig.* What has my poverty got to do with you?

*Apic.* Nothing at all, and I should not like it to concern
me. But to work! And outside of work let
us have no more talk than necessary. Are
my orders not sufficient? Nothing apparently
can be enough for you in the way of closely
laying down and insisting over and over again
on what is to be done. Give me my cooking-
trousers. I want to go out of doors, but I will
soon be back. Give me also, please, the olive-
crusher (*tudicula*), the badge of our art. This
is my thunderbolt and trident.

*Pist.* Hallo, Abligurinus, place those jugs on the urn-
table and wash this beef steadily, and give it a
good rubbing in the basin.

*Ablig.* Have you any other orders to give? One com-
mander is sufficient for one camp, but it does
not seem to be sufficient for one kitchen. Do
it all yourself. You are a sharper exactor of
work than the master of the cook-shop himself. For the future I won't call you Pistillarius (a pounder with the pestle), but a sharp
sting (*stimulus acutus*).

*Pist.* Nay, rather call me *Onocentron* (the spur of
asses). Cut up then this calf's flesh on this
flesh-board. Also powder the cheese so that
we can sprinkle it over this dumpling.

*Ablig.* How? With the hand?

*Pist.* No, but with the grater. Pour a few drops of oil
in from the cruse.

*Ablig.* Do you mean from this flask?

*Pist.* Place here the mortar.

*Ablig.* Which of them?

*Pist.* That brazen one with the pestle of the same metal.

*Ablig.* What for?

*Pist.* For grinding rock-parsley.

*Ablig.* This is done more satisfactorily in a marble
mortar with a wooden pestle.


### III. *Songs*

*Pist.* Please sing us a song, as you are wont to do.

*Ablig.*

> Ego nolo Caesar esse,
> Ambulare per Britannos,
> Scythicas pati pruinas.[1]
> FLORUS.[2]

> Ut sapiant fatuae Fabiorum prandia betae,
> O quam saepe petet vina piperque coquus.[3]
> MARTIAL'S *Epigrams*, 13, 13.

*Pist.* Do you say the *Fabii* or the *fabri?*

*Ablig.* On that point inquire of the bandy-legged schoolmaster and you will get for your *Fabii* and
*fabri* a sound blow on the cheek or the back.

*Pist.* Is that the sort of man?

*Ablig.* He is a determined, courageous man, prompt
with blows. He compensates for the slowness
of his tongue by the swiftness of his hands.

---

[1] I am not willing to be Caesar, to march through the Britons
and to suffer Scythian frosts.

[2] So says Aelius Spartianus in *Life of Hadrian Florus* as quoted
by Freigius. See *Crinitus*, book 15, cap. 5.

[3] How often the cook seeks pepper and wine for the break-
fasts of the Fabii to smack of the simple beet.

*Pist.* Here, bring the beer-jug. My palate, throat, gullet are parched with thirst.

*Ablig.*

Et gravis attrita pendebat cantharus ansa.[1]
> VERGIL, *Eclogue*, 6, 17.

Claudere quae coenas lactuca solebat avorum,
Dic mihi, cur nostros inchoat illa dapes? [2]
> MARTIAL, *Epigram*, 13, 14.

Filia Picenae venio Lucanica porcae,
Pultibus hinc niveis grata corona datur.[3]
> MARTIAL, *Epigram*, 13, 35.

*Apic.* Where hast thou thus learnt to ῥαψωδεῖν?

*Ablig.* Lately I served a schoolmaster in Calabria who was a poetaster. He often used to give me no other meal than a song of a hundred verses, in which he used to say there was a wonderful savour. I, indeed, would rather have had a little bread and cheese. There was, however, enough water for the house, and we had permission to drink from the well to our heart's content. If I then had gone hungry to bed, instead of food I chewed those verses and digested them. Nor did there seem to me to be any other remedy to drive away the keenness of hunger (*bulimia*) than to betake myself to the art of cookery.

*Apic.* What services did you render that schoolmaster?

*Ablig.* Such as Caesar rendered to the Republic. I was

---

[1] And heavily used to hang on his arm a bowl with a worn-out handle.

[2] Tell me why does the lettuce, which used to finish off the meals of our ancestors, now begin *our* meals?

[3] When I, the Lucanian sausage, come, daughter of the swine of Picenum, then will the crown be given gladly to the snowy pottage.

everything to him. I was his counsellor, though he had nothing to advise about; he had nothing secret from me, not even in his personal habits. I used to pour water on his hand, which he never used to wash himself. I served him as his treasurer.

*Apic.* What treasure had he?

*Ablig.* He had a few sheets of the trashiest poems which the moths used to eat away and barbarian mice gnawed at.

*Apic.* Nay, say learned mice, since they bit their teeth into bad poems.

# XVI

## TRICLINIUM—*The Dining-room*

### ARISTIPPUS, LURCO

This dialogue is connected with the two following dialogues. For this contains descriptions of the master of a feast and his dining-room, the next of the banquet itself, and the third, drunkenness. It has two parts—the introduction and description (*narratio*). Triclinium is so called from having three dining-couches (*lectus*). For, of old, those about to breakfast or dine were accustomed to arrange couches for lying on, for the most part three. *See* Castilionius in book 6; Vitruvius, cap. 5; Baysius de Vasculis. Aristippus was the disciple of Socrates, from whom was derived the Cyrenaic teaching. For he lived in ease, sumptuously, voluptuously. He sought out every luxury of perfumes, clothes, women, and counted life happy in so far as it was full of pleasure.

παριόντα ποτε αὐτὸν λάχανα πλύνων Διογένης
ἔσκωψε καὶ φησιν : εἰ ταῦτα ἔμαθες προσφέρεοθαι
οὐκ ἂν τυράννων αὐλὰς ἐθεράπευες. Ὁ δέ, καὶ σύ, εἶπεν,
εἴπερ ᾔδεις ἀνθρώποις ὁμιλεῖν, οὐκ ἂν λάχανα ἔπλυνες.[1]

DIOG. LAERT. i. 68.

## I. *The Introduction* (*Initium*)

*Arist.* Why are you so late getting up and, indeed, still half-asleep?

*Lurc.* I am surprised that I have waked up at all the whole of this day, since yesterday we were eating and drinking.

[1] As he passed by one day, Diogenes, who was washing vegetables, scoffed at him and said: " It you had learnt to live on these, you would not frequent the courts of kings; " and he said: " If you knew how to associate with your fellow men, you would not be washing vegetables."

125

*Arist.* Nay, as it appears, you were simply gorging, gourmandising, and overwhelming yourself with sumptuous dishes and wine. But where was it you were thus loading your swift-sailing ship?

*Lurc.* At the house of Scopas, at a banquet (*convivium*).

*Arist.* Nay, rather, according to the manner of the Greeks, call it a συμπόσιον than by the Latin word *convivium*.

*Lurc.* One brawler aroused another to speech. Olives and sauces pricked and pinched the sated stomach, and would not let the appetite get wearied out.

*Arist.* Pray tell us all the courses so that by hearing of them I can imagine that I was there, and as if I were drinking with you, as that man who ate two great loaves of bread in a Spanish inn, and enjoyed the exhalation of a roasted partridge, in place of further viands.

*Lurc.* Who could tell all? This would be a greater undertaking than to have bought the food, or prepared it, ør what would have beaten everything in difficulty, to have eaten it all up.

*Arist.* Let us sit down here in this willow-plantation, by the bank of this little stream, and, since we are tired, let us talk of your yesterday's dining out, instead of other things. The grass will serve us for bolsters. Lean on that elm-tree.

*Lurc.* On the grass? Won't the moisture harm us?

*Arist.* How stupid! moisture, when the dog-star is rising!

*Lurc.* Formerly I refused; now my mind desires to tell

you yet more than you ask. You inquire from
me as to the banquet; you shall also hear as
to the host and the dining-room. You asked
that I would speak; I will do so that, soon
perhaps, you will ask, proclaim, command
silence, as was the case with the Arabian flute-
player who was induced to sing for an *obolus*,
but was only brought to silence by receiving
three.

*Arist.* Say as much as thou wishest of the feast; I shall
not be pained by it, since we are now sitting in
a shady place, and the goldfinch there accom-
panies thy narrative, or at least will bring
harmony into it, as the slaves with the flute
did into the speech of C. Gracchus.[1]

## II. *Narration—Description of Scopas*

*Lurc.* What was that story?

*Arist.* When you have finished your account of the
feast you shall have the story of the *Gracchi*,
of the *graculi*,[2] and the *Graeculi*.

*Lurc.* We were going for a walk by chance across
the market (*forum*), Thrasybulus and I. We
happened to have got more leisure than is
usual with us. Scopas joined us. When he
had made his first salutations, and started a
suave conversation, Scopas began earnestly to

---

[1] *See* Cicero, *De Oratore*, iii. (near the end); Quintilian, i. 10;
Gellius, *Noctes Atticae*, i. 11.

[2] *Graculus* is a jackdaw. Aesop has a story of the jackdaw
with borrowed plumes. Juvenal iii. 78 refers to the *Graeculus*,
the Roman attempting to play the Greek.

entreat us that we would, on the next day, which was yesterday, go to his house. First we excused ourselves, the one for one reason, the other for another; I, on account of an important engagement with a magistrate (*praetor*), a very irritable gentleman. But Scopas, a man who likes to boast of his wealth, began an elaborate speech, as if his life were in question. What need of further words? We said yes, so that he should not continue to worry us.

*Arist.* Do you know why he arranged the banquet?

*Lurc.* What was it, pray, do you suppose?

*Arist.* He is indeed himself a rich man, well provided with silver, clothes, and house-provisions. But he had bought three gilded silver phials and six cups. These would have lost their value to him, had he not invited some guests to whom he might show them. For he believes that it is in the ostentation of wealth that its pleasure consists. He is driven on to profuse expenditure by his wife, who calls it magnificence.

### Description of the Dining-hall

*Lurc.* Yesterday, then, about mid-day we came together to his dining-room.

*Arist.* What kind of a lunch was it?

*Lurc.* In the open air, in the cool shade. All was splendidly prepared, decorated, polished up. Nothing was lacking in elegance, splendour,

and magnificence. Immediately on entrance,
our eyes and souls were exhilarated by the
most beautiful and most pleasant sights.
There was a great sideboard, full of beautiful
vases of all kinds, of gold, silver, crystal, glass,
ivory, myrrh-wood; also others of more
common material, tin, horn, bone, wood, shell,
or earthenware, in which art lent a merit
to the commonness of the material, for there
were very many pieces of embossed work,
all brightly cleaned and polished; the glitter
almost dazzled the eyes. You might have seen
there two great silver wash-hand-basins with
gilded borders. The middle part together with
the ornaments about it were of gold. Every
basin had its outlet whose bung was gilded.
There stood there also another water-basin of
glass, similarly with gilded pipe, as well as an
earthenware wash-basin varnished with red
*sandarach*,[1] a piece of work of the Spanish city
of Malaca. Besides, there were phials of
every kind and two silver ones for the most
generous kind of wines.

*Arist.* From my own experience I prefer flasks of glass
or of shells, which they call stone-ware.

*Lurc.* What are you to do? Such is the nature of man!
He does not in these things seek so much
convenience as the opinion of being thought
rich.

*Arist.* These very rich people pretty often seem so to
others whilst to themselves they seem poor.

[1] A red colouring matter.

So there is no end of bringing forward, and presenting, to the eyes of others, their possessions. Especially is this so with those who have no other kind of skill in which they can trust. But proceed.

*Lurc.* The border of the sideboard was covered with a shaggy carpet brought from Turkey. At a distance from the sideboard there were placed two small tables with quadrants and silver orbs. Every one had his salt-cellar, knife, bread, and napkin. Under the sideboard stood a refrigerator and large wine-decanters. Then they had various kinds of seats, settles, double-seats, benches, and the seat of the lady of the house, arranged so as to fold up, a noteworthy piece of work with silken upholstery, and provided with a foot-stool.

*Arist.* Lay the table now, and unfold the napkins, for my vitals cry out for hunger.

*Lurc.* The dining-table was large. It was inlaid with ancient mosaic work. It had belonged to the Prince Dicæarchus.

*Arist.* O old table, what a different master is yours now!

*Lurc.* He had bought the table at an auction sale at a sufficiently high price, only because it had belonged to the prince, and he would thus have something that had been his. Water is given for the washing of hands. At first there are great mutual refusings and invitations and yielding by turns.

*Arist.* The same thing happened in all this yielding of dignity, when each one made himself of less

account than the other, and exalted the other
with the haughtiest courteousness, whilst in
reality every one thought himself more important than all the rest.

*Lurc.* But the host, by his own right, allotted the seats.
Grace was said by a little boy briefly and per-
functorily, but not without rhythm :—

Quod appositum est et apponetur, Christus benedicere dignetur.[1]

Each one unfolds his napkin and throws it over
the left shoulder.   Then he cleans his bread
with his knife, in case he did not think it had
been sufficiently cleaned by the servant, for it
had been placed before him with the crust
taken off.

*Arist.* Did you sit in ease ?

*Lurc.* Never with more ease.

*Arist.* You couldn't get a poor lunch.   For the eatables
had been supplied to redundancy, so far as
ever the market had them ;  this I know.

*Lurc.* In no place has this more certainly happened.
But the very abundance palled.   The director
of the table busied himself with laying knives
and forks.   Then came in, with great pomp,
the chief steward with a long band of boys,
younger and older, who bore away the dishes
of the first course.

[1] On what has been set and is set before us, may Christ deign
to give his blessing.

# XVII

## CONVIVIUM—*The Banquet*

Scopas, Simonides, Crito, Democritus, Polaemon

Concerning Scopas, *see* Cicero, book 2, *de Orat*. As to Polaemon, *see* Val. Max. bk. 6, cap. 11. There are three kinds of banquets, εἰλαπίνη, a magnificent and splendid banquet; γάμος, a nuptial banquet; and ἔρανος, when each guest came at his own expense and brought his own food. Homer links together those forms of banquets: εἰλαπίνη ἠὲ γάμος; ἐπεὶ οὐκ ἔρανος τάδε γ᾽ἐστί (*Odyssea*, i. 226).

The parts of this dialogue are these: Initium, apparatus, finis. Apparatus contains two courses.

### COURSES

|       |       |          |          |
|-------|-------|----------|----------|
| First | Cibus | Panis    |          |
|       |       | Obsonia  | Carnes   |
|       |       |          | Pultes   |
|       |       |          | Pisces   |
|       | Potus | Vinum    |          |
|       |       | Aqua     |          |
|       |       | Cerevisia|          |
|       |       | Pocula   |          |
| Second|       | Fructus  |          |
|       |       | Casei    |          |
|       |       | Tragemata|          |

## I. *The Beginning (Initium)*

*Scop.* Where is our Simonides?

*Crit.* He said he would come immediately after he had met a debtor of his in the market.

*Scop.* He does rightly. He will more easily get away from a debtor than he would from a creditor.

*Crit.* How is this?

*Scop.* It is as in a victory, the victor imposes the conditions, not the vanquished. The debtor comes away from the creditor when he will, the creditor when the debtor is willing. But have you not all met, as you arranged, and left the seriousness of home, bringing with you cheerfulness, wit, grace, pleasantness?

*Crit.* Clearly these things are so, I hope, and we will be as M. Varro advises, an agreeable company.

*Scop.* Let the rest be my concern.

*Crit.* Here is Simonides coming!

*Scop.* Happy event!

*Sim.* All prosperity to you!

*Scop.* We have keenly desired you!

*Sim.* Ah, how boorish it all is! But you see I was invited to lunch, not for a period of detention in business. But have I really kept you waiting long?

*Scop.* No, indeed not.

*Sim.* Why did you not set to the meal without me? At least you could have begun with the fruit which I am not much given to eating.

*Scop.* Courteous words, but how could we sit down without you?

## II. *First Course—Bread*

*Crit.* Enough of civilities. Let us begin our description. The best and lightest of bread! It is as light in weight as a sponge. The wheat is soft as a medlar. You must have an industrious miller.

*Scop.* Roscius has the mill in his charge.

*Sim.* Is he never hurled into it?

*Scop.* Far be such a fate from such a thrifty servant!

*Dem.* Pass me the coarse bread (made of unbolted flour).

*Sim.* And me the bread made of the middle quality of foreign wheat.

*Scop.* Why do you wish that?

*Sim.* Because I have both heard and found from experience that I eat less when the bread has not a fine taste.

*Scop.* Here, boy, bring him common bread, and even the black bread if he prefers. We will have the most pleasant of meals, if every one shall take what most pleases him.

*Pol.* This bread, which you praise so much, is spongy, watery; I prefer it thicker.

*Crit.* I indeed don't dislike it spongy—so long as it isn't hastily made. But this also has cracks such as cakes baked on the hearth are accustomed to have, although, as is sufficiently clear, this came out of the oven.

*Pol.* This black bread is both sour and full of chaff; you would say that it was from flour of second-rate wheat.

*Scop.* So our husbandmen are accustomed to do with all wheat which they bring hither; first to make it pungent with the common, and to mix it with all kinds of seeds; the taste then comes from the leaven being excessive.

*Pol.* No class of men are more deceptive than husbandmen. They only act wrongly through ignorance.

*Crit.* This bread is not sufficiently fermented.

*Dem.* For to-day think thyself a Jew, one of those who,
by the ordinance of God, only feed on bread
which is unleavened.

*Crit.* And this, indeed, was because they were such
very bad men that the eating of swine was forbidden them, than which nothing is more
pleasing to the palate; nor if taken moderately
is anything more healthful. With unleavened
bread sauces must be eaten together with
field lettuce, which is extremely bitter.

*Pol.* All this has too much depth of meaning. Let us
leave the subject.

*Scop.* Yes, indeed, and the whole discussion about
bread! If there is so much difference of
opinion about what is eaten with bread, how
much discord there will be over every part of
the menu of the whole meal!

*Crit.* It happens, forsooth, as Horace says:—

> Tres mihi convivae prope dissentire videntur,
> Poscentes vario multum diversa palato.[1]

### Fruits

*Scop.* Bring those dishes and plates with the cherries,
plums, pomegranates, ripe fruit, and early ripe
fruit.

---

[1] Even with three guests, each seems to me to have a different
taste, each requiring quite different foods with his quite different
palate. HORACE, *Epistles*, ii. 2, 61, 62.

*Pol.* Why did Varro say that the number of guests
ought not to exceed the number of the Muses,
when the number of the Muses is not settled?
For some put the number at three; others six;
others nine.

*Crit.* He spoke as if it were established that there were
nine, and so it was commonly accepted.
Whence Diogenes made his joke at the expense of the schoolmaster, who had only a
small number of scholars in the school, whilst
he had the Muses painted on the walls. The
master, said he, has many scholars, if you
reckon in the Muses (σὺν ταῖς μούσαις).

*Dem.* But is it true that the Persians introduced into
Greece the fruit which they regarded as so
deadly as to be a pestilence to those against
whom they were waging war?

*Crit.* So I have heard.

*Dem.* How wonderful is the variety of products in the
different nature of soils!

*Crit.* India sends ivory, says Vergil,[1] the effeminate
Sabaeans their frankincense. Oh! look at
those Persian quinces!

*Sim.* This is a new kind of grafting which the ancients
did not know of. Reach me the bowl with the
hard-skinned figs, which are, as you know,
early ripe.

*Scop.* Enough of the fruits! Let us be filled with more
healthful foods of the body.

*Crit.* What is, then, healthier?

*Scop.* Nothing, if to be health-giving and of good

[1] *Georgics,* i. 57.

taste are the same thing as in a mid-day
dream.

*Crit.* I forgive fruits their harmfulness on account of
their pleasantness of taste.

### Meats

*Scop.* Do you remember the verse of Cato?

    Pauca voluptati debentur; plura saluti.[1]

Give every one a platter of meat with sauce, so
that he may swallow it down, and this will
warm the intestines and pleasantly wash and
so soften the body.

*Sim.* Here, boy, give me at once some salted pork. Oh!
most savoury leg of pork! It is a barrow-
hog. If you can hear what I say, return
the cabbage and bacon, to the cook, at this
season of the year, or preserve it till the
winter. Cut me a couple of bits off this
sausage, so that the first cup of wine may taste
the sweeter.

*Crit.* Let us follow the advice of physicians that wine
be taken with pork. Pour out wine.

### Wine

*Scop.* Now follows action after talk. Surely this is
wisest at this time of the year. Look at
the necessary preparations for our drinking
wine. First of all the keeper of the sideboard

---

[1] We should give little to pleasure, as its due; but all the
more to health. CATO, *Disticha de Moribus*, ii. 28.

(*custos abaci*) has set out the cups of brightest crystal glass with purest white wine; you would think it water by its mere appearance. It is San Martin wine and partly Rhein wine, but not mixed as they are accustomed to drink it in Belgium, but such as they drink in mid-Germany. The wine-seller to-day has tapped two casks, one of yellow Helvell from the neighbourhood of Paris, and one of blood-red Bordeaux. Others are in readiness kept cool, dark (*fuscus*) from Aquitaine and black from Saguntum. Let every one choose according to his liking.

*Crit.* What suggestion could be more delightful? as nothing is harder fortune than to perish of thirst. For myself I should prefer that you had set before us the best water. I would rather have heard such an announcement than that of the wines.

*Scop.* Nor shall that be lacking.

*Sim.* Lately when I was in Rome, I drank at a cardinal's house, the noblest wines of every flavour; sweet, sharp, mild, fruity, and tart. I was indeed extremely friendly with the wine-cellarer.

*Dem.* I dearly like fiery wine.

*Pol.* So also do Belgian women. In some places in France they offer you the dregs of wine. They most delight in two and three year old vintage. But these are rather sampling of wine than real wine-drinking, and French wine especially bears neither the addition of water

# Convivium

nor years. Therefore soon after it is racked off
it is drunk. Indeed, in a year it begins to get
worse, and becomes uncertain, then its flavour
escapes and it becomes sour. Had it been
kept longer it would become mouldy and flat.
The Spanish and Italian wines, on the other
hand, improve with age, and with the addition
of water.

*Dem.* What do you mean by wine getting " flat "?
The casks become shrunken, the wine is
enclosed in cells, and the casing of the cask
falls in, if need be.

*Pol.* Like as fruit gets uneatable through decay by age
and does not keep, and, as we say commonly,
goes bad. The opposite term is " still wine "
(*consistens*).

*Dem.* Pour me first a half-cupful of water and then
pour in the wine, after the old custom.

*Crit.* Nay, to-day's custom is yet the same with many
people, the French and Germans being excep-
tions.

*Dem.* The nations who drink water with wine pour wine
to the water; those who will drink wine
watered, pour water on to the wine.

*Crit.* And what do those drink who mix no water with
their wine?

*Dem.* Pure, unmixed wine.

*Crit.* That is, if the wine-dealer did not first water it
himself.

*Pol.* They call that baptising it, so that the wine should
be Christian. This was in my time a fine,
philosophical way of speaking.

*Dem.* They baptise the wine, and themselves are un-
baptised (*i.e.*, unwatered or unwashed).

*Pol.* They do worse to wine who add chalk, sulphur,
honey, alum, and other more noisome things
than which nothing is more pernicious to one's
body.  Against such people the state ought to
proceed as against robbers or assassins.  For
thence are incredible kinds of diseases and
especially gout.

*Crit.* By conspiracy with physicians they can do this.
Then both share the profit.

*Dem.* The cup you reach to me is too full.  Empty it a
little, I beg, so that there may be a space for
water.

### Drinking

*Crit.* Pour me wine in that chestnut-coloured cup.
What is that?

*Scop.* A great Indian nut, surrounded with a silver edge.
Won't you drink out of that bowl of ebony
wood?  They say that this is the healthiest.
But don't give me too much water.  Don't
you know the old proverb: " You spoil wine
when you pour water into it "?

*Dem.* Yes, then you spoil both the water and the wine.

*Pol.* I would rather spoil both, than be spoiled by one
of them.

*Scop.* Would it not be pleasant, according to the Greek
custom, to drink out of the bowls and from
the bigger beakers?

*Pol.* By no means.  You reminded us just now of the
old proverb.  In my turn I remind you of the

Pauline precept: " Be not drunk with wine, wherein is excess "; and that of our Saviour: " And take heed to yourselves lest at any time your hearts be overcharged with surfeiting and drunkenness."

### Water

*Crit.* Whence is this cold water, so pure and pellucid?

*Scop.* Out of the spring near by here.

*Crit.* Rather than mixing of wine I prefer cistern water, if it is thoroughly pure.

*Dem.* What do you think of spring-drawn water?

*Crit.* It is more appropriate for washing purposes than for drinking.

*Pol.* Very many people commend flowing water.

*Crit.* And quite rightly if the streams flow through gold veins, as in Spain, and the water is peaceful and clear.

### Beer

*Sim.* Bring me in that Samian phial some beer which, in this heat, should be very good for refreshing one's body.

*Scop.* Which sort of beer will you have?

*Sim.* The lightest you have, for other kinds muddle the mind too much and make the body too fat.

*Pol.* Give me some also, but in the round glass.

*Scop.* Run to the kitchen and see what they are waiting for. Why don't they send another course? You see that already no one further tastes of this. Bring young cocks cooked with lettuce, garden oxtongue, and endive; also mutton and calf's flesh.

*Crit.* Add also a little mustard or rock-parsley in small dishes.

*Dem.* Mustard seems to me a strong (*violenta*) food.

*Crit.* It is not suitable for bilious people, but is not without its usefulness for those who abound in thick and cold humours.

*Pol.* Therefore are the countries of northern latitudes wise in using it, for whom it is of great service, especially with thick and hard food, *e.g.*, with beef and salted fish.

### Pottage

*Scop.* In this place, I think broth and rice come seasonably, also ash - coloured bread, fine wheaten bread, starch-food, rice, " little worms " (*vermiculi*). Let every one take according to his taste.

*Dem.* I have seen those who shuddered terribly at " little worms " because they believed they were out of the earth and from mud, and had previously been alive.

*Crit.* Such people deserve to have these " worms " come to life again in their stomachs. They say that rice is born in water and dies in wine. Give me, therefore, wine.

*Dem.* Drink not immediately after warm food. Eat first something cold and solid.

*Crit.* What?

*Dem.* A crust of bread, or a rissole or two of meat.

### Fish

*Sim.* Bah! fish and meat at the same sitting! To mix earth and sea. This is forbidden by physicians.

*Scop.* Nay, rather physicians are pleased by it.

*Sim.* I think it is because it is profitable to them.

*Scop.* Why, then, do the physicians forbid it?

*Sim.* I have made a mistake. I ought to have said that it is prohibited by the art of medicine, not by physicians. But what sort of fish is this?

*Scop.* Place them in order. The first is roasted pike with vinegar and capers, then turbot cooked with the juice of pointed sorrel, fried soles, a fresh pike and a *capito* (large-headed fish)— the salted pike serve for yourself—fresh roasted and salted tunny-fish, fresh *maenae* (small sea fish) fried, pasties, in which are many bearded-fishes, *murenae*, and trout, with suitable relishes, fried gudgeon and boiled lobsters and crabs. Mingle with them dishes with garlic, pepper, mustard, pounded up.

*Sim.* I will indeed speak of the fish, but not eat of them.

*Crit.* If a philosopher begins to conduct a controversy on fish, *i.e.*, on a most uncertain, debatable question, then let us have a bed set up, so that we can sleep here.

*Scop.* No one is worthy to even taste these dishes. Take them away.

*Sim.* And yet formerly banquets at Rome were most

splendid and they were accustomed to say that sumptuous ones were given which consisted entirely of fish.

*Crit.* Thus have times changed, although this custom also lasts with some people.

### Birds

*Scop.* Bring up roasted chickens, partridges, thrushes, ducklings, teal, wood-pigeons, rabbits, hares, calf's flesh, kids, and sauce or flavours, vinegar, oil, fruit penetrating in its medical properties, also citrons, olives from the Balearic Islands, preserved, pressed, and kept in pickle.

*Dem.* Are no Bethica (district of Spain) olives there?

*Scop.* Those from the Balearic Islands taste better.

*Crit.* What will happen to those big animals there, the goose, the swan, the peacock?

*Scop.* Merely show them, and take them back to the kitchen.

*Pol.* See there a peacock! Where is Q. Hortensius who held a peacock for such a delicacy?[1]

*Sim.* Take the lamb-meat away.

*Scop.* Why?

*Sim.* Because it is unsound. They say it does not go out by any other way than that it entered.

*Crit.* I have seen someone who swallowed olive stones like an ostrich.

*Scop.* From what meat are those pasties made?

*Crit.* This here is stag's flesh.

[1] *See* Varro, *De re rustica*, III. vi. 6.

*Scop.* This is deer's flesh; and that there, I believe, is boar's flesh.

*Crit.* I prefer the condiments to meat itself.

*Sim.* And that is clearly right, for spice renders the sourest things sweet.

*Crit.* What is the spice of the whole of life?

*Dem.* An equable mind.

*Crit.* I can name something else, which is of larger scope and more august.

*Dem.* What can be more important than what I have named?

*Crit. Pietas,* under which equanimity is included. Moreover, "piety" is the most suitable and pleasant sauce for all things hard and easy, and those things which lie between these extremes.

*Scop.* Pour white Spanish wine in that beaker and bear it round to the guests.

*Dem.* What are you preparing to do? When dinner is finished, bring us some strong and generous wine. We can afterwards drink something more diluted, if we wish to take care of our health.

*Sim.* Thy counsel seems to me good, for it behoves us to have colder food at the end of a meal, which by its weight may thrust down the other food to the bottom of the stomach, and may restrain the vapours from escaping to the head.

### III. *Second Course*

*Scop.* Take away those things; change the round and square plates, and lay the second table (dessert). For no one is anywhere further stretching forth his hand to the dishes.

*Crit.* I have eaten so heartily from the beginning that I have quite lost all further appetite.

*Dem.* I also have no more appetite, but I was led on by the desire of the fruit dishes here, and so have eaten to satiety.

*Pol.* I have eaten I don't know how much fish. This has repulsed all my appetite.

*Sim.* And is there so much of splendid dainties and delicacies before us when there is no longer the desire of eating? Pears, apples, and cheese of many kinds! The most attractive to my palate is the horse-cheese.

*Crit.* I believe that it is not horse-cheese at all, but Phrygian cheese from asses' milk, such as is brought from Sicily in the form of columns and squares. When one is broken, it cleaves into layers or, as it were, sheets (of paper).

*Dem.* This cheese is porous as if it were from England, and will not in my opinion be pleasing to you.

*Crit.* Nor will this spongy Dutch cheese. This from Parma is thicker and, as it seems, fairly fresh, and that Penasellian (Spanish) will easily vie with it.

*Dem.* This cheese is not from Parma but Placentia.

*Crit.* It also is pleasant. Commonly the cheese dearest to the Germans is old cheese, putrid, fried up and wormy.

*Sim.* He who eats such cheese is hunting for thirst and he eats in order to drink.

*Scop.* The pastry-cook delays too long with his sweets.
Why does he not bring his tarts, his wine-
cakes and cup-cakes and the fried cakes made
of a concoction thrown into a vessel of boiling
oil with honey poured over it?

*Crit.* Give me a few dates, both some to eat and some
to keep by me. Perhaps I shall to-night eat
nothing else.

*Scop.* Then take the whole of this branch of them.
Will you have some pomegranates?

*Pol.* Here, boy, relieve me of these wild dates and give
me something eatable.

*Scop.* I advise you to drink. Don't you know that it
was the opinion of Aristotle that the dessert
was introduced into meals to invite us to drinking lest the food should be digested dry?

*Crit.* The discoverer must have been either a sailor or
fish to be so much afraid of dryness.

*Scop.* Take away those things which are ordinarily called
the seal of the stomach, because after them
nothing more is to be eaten or drunk, biscuits,
quince - cakes, coriander covered with sugar.
But such food must be chewed, not eaten.
What remains from the portion chewed must
be spit out, for it is uneatable. Collect the
bits and what remains over in baskets; bring
scented waters, of rose, of the flowers of the
healing apple (citron), and of musk-melon.

## IV. *End of the Banquet*

*Pol.* Let us return thanks to Christ.

*The Boy.*

> Agimus tibi gratias, Pater, qui tam multa ad hom-
> inum usus condidisti: annue, ut tuo favore ad coenam
> illam veniamus tuae beatitudinis.[1]

*Pol.* Now then let us return thanks to the host.

*Crit.* Well, you do it.

*Pol.* Nay, rather Democritus, who is strong on these
points.

*Dem.* I cannot return thanks as in duty bound to thee,
deserving well of the republic, for all has been
confused by Bacchus, but I will recite what
once Diogenes said to Dionysius; I have committed his speech to memory. If I have a
lapse of memory or a faltering tongue you will
forgive me after so great a soaking of drink.

*Scop.* Say what you will; it will be written in wine.

*Dem.* Thou hast, my Scopas, thyself, thy wife, thy
man-servants and maid-servants, neighbours,
cooks, and pastry-cooks, wearied thyself and
themselves, so that we may become yet more
wearied by eating and drinking. When
Socrates had entered a very crowded market,
he exclaimed wisely, " O immortal gods, how
many things there are here which I don't
need." Thou, on the contrary, mightest say,
" What a small part is all this of that which I
need." The idea of moderation is pleasing to
Nature. Thereon it is formed and supported.
This supply of many and manifold things over-

---

[1] We render thanks to Thee, Father, who has provided so many
things for the enjoyment of men: Grant that, by Thy good-will,
we may come to the feast of Thy Blessedness.

whelms Nature, as Pliny rightly observes. Manifoldness of food is injurious to man; yet more injurious is every sauce. We take hence to our homes bodies made heavy by these things, minds oppressed and sunk in food and drinks, so that we cannot duly perform any human duty. Do you yourself point out what thanks we owe you.

*Scop.* Are these the thanks you have for me? Thus you pay back so splendid a meal!

*Pol.* Clearly it is so—for what greater benefit is there than becoming wiser? You send us home evidently beasts. We wish to leave you at home a man, so that you may know how to consult your own health and that of others and to live conformably to the desires of Nature, not following fancies caught up from folly. Farewell and learn wisdom.

# XVIII

## EBRIETAS—*Drunkenness*

### Asotus, Tricongius, Abstemius, Glaucia

In this dialogue Vives describes the causes and effects of drunkenness. The occasion of the dialogue is based on Horace, book i. Epist. 5, where firstly is described the desire to cast away care by a splendid feast, to drink the best wines freely and in quantities, for Horace says:

> Potare et spargere flores
> Incipiam patiarque vel inconsultus haberi.

Then he adds the seven effects of drunkenness. It causes the disclosure of secrets, renders men confident, makes them bold, takes away anxiety, brings the fatuous impression of wisdom, makes men garrulous and loquacious, and in the depth of poverty renders men dissolute and lavish.

> Quid non ebrietas designat? operta recludit:
> Spes jubet esse ratas, in praelia trudit inermem.
> Sollicitis animis onus eximit, addocet artes.
> Foecundi calices quem non fecêre disertum?
> Contractâ quem non in paupertate solutum?

Here, again, names of interlocutors are aptly applied. Asotus (middle vowel long) is a man given up to luxuries of the palate. In Latin such is called *heluo* (glutton), *nepos* (spendthrift), *decoctor* (bankrupt). The Greek word comes from a privative particle, and σώζω; Latin, *servo*. *See* Cicero, book 2, *de Finibus :* "Nolim asotos, qui in mensam vomant, et qui de conviviis auferantur, crudique nostridie se rursus ingurgitent; qui solem (ut aiunt) nec occidentem unquam viderint, nec orientem: qui consumtis patrimoniis egeant. Nemo istius generis asotos jucunde putat vivere."

Concerning Tricongius we have spoken in the dialogue "Garrientes." Abstemius is one who does not drink wine, as if held back, *i.e.* from wine. There are two parts to the dialogue, the Exordium, which contains the occasion of the dialogue, and Narratio, the telling of the story.

## I. *Exordium*

*Asot.* What do you say, Tricongius? How splendidly
that Brabantian entertained us yesterday!

*Tric.* A curse on him, for I could not rest the whole
night! I was sick, with all due respect to
you let me say it (*sit habitus honos vestris
auribus*), and then tossed myself about all over
the bed, now on the inner, then on the outer,
frame of the bed. It seemed to me as if I
should vomit forth throat and stomach. Even
now I cannot use my eyes or ears for headache.
It is as if I had heavy bars of lead lying on my
forehead and eyes.

*Asot.* Fasten a band round your forehead and temples,
and you will seem to be a king.

*Tric.* Much rather like Bacchus himself, from whom the
institution of diadems on kings was derived.

*Asot.* Go home, then, and sleep off the soaking.

*Tric.* Home, indeed! There is no place I should shun
so much as my home. I should feel too much
aversion to meet my shrieking wife. For if
she were to see me now she would entertain
me with longer homilies than Chrysostom.

*Abstem.* And this is what you call being treated
splendidly!

*Glauc.* Clearly so; for your throat and stomach have
been well washed!

*Abstem.* And the hands too?

*Glauc.* Not even once.

*Asot.* Nay, on the contrary, often with wine and milk,

whilst we dipped our hands in one another's bowls (*pateras*).

*Glauc.* What could be said more splendidly? Fancy the fingers sticking with the fat of meat and with sauces.

*Abstem.* By the gods, keep quiet! Who could listen without nausea to the unclean business, much less look upon it, or taste of such wine or milk.

*Asot.* By your faith, ye gods! are you so delicate a man, Abstemius, that you cannot swallow this even with your ears? What would you do with your palate, if you were like us? But listen to me, Tricongius, sweetest fellow-wine-bibber, let us send some boy to fetch us some of the same wine in that clay vessel. There is no surer antidote against this poison.

*Tric.* Has this been tried?

*Asot.* Why should it not be so? Don't you remember the verses which Colax sings:—

> Ad sanandum morsum canis nocturni,
> Sume ex pilis eiusdem canis.[1]
>
> PLAUTUS.

*Glauc.* Tell us, I beg you, all about the banquet.

*Abstem.* Nay, don't! unless you wish me to part with all I have in my stomach, and even the vitals themselves.

*Glauc.* Then go away for a short time.

*Asot.* I will tell you as frankly as possible, but so as nowhere to go beyond the limits of decency.

[1] For getting well from the bite of dog at night, take from the dog's hair your remedy.

*Glauc.* Begin, I beseech you. Give your attention, Abstemius.

*Asot.* My dear Glaucia, before everything, I am of opinion that there is no class of men which can be likened to festive and liberal hosts at banquets. Some show knowledge of all kinds of things, *i.e.*, of mere trifles; others show with pride, experience, and wisdom gathered from practice. And what of this? There are people who indeed have wealth, but, wretched that they are, they don't dare to spend it. What they have, they take pleasure in storing up. A kindly host is everywhere of use, everywhere is welcome. The very sight of him is sufficient to heal the sadness of the mind and scatter it; and if a man has any wretchedness, the memory of the feast takes it away. So, too, does the hope and expectation of a coming feast. All the other so-called mental blessings I don't care to look on; they are, to me, slight and unfruitful.

*Abstem.* I ask you, Asotus, who is the author of such a fine sentiment?

*Asot.* I and all like me, *i.e.*, a host of people from Belgic France, from the Seine to the Rhine. There are only a few poor and very sparing men who think differently, who envy Abstemius his name, and wish to be called frugal, or else certain distinguished people who are puffed up with a great opinion of their own wisdom, *i.e.*, an empty word, whom we (*i.e.*, the greatest and chief part of mankind) simply laugh at.

*Abstem.* What do I hear?

## Digression

*Glauc.* He is quite right, though he is drunk. For nowhere has scholarship less estimation than in Belgium. A distinguished man in scholarship is not otherwise esteemed than one who is occupied in shoe-making or in weaving.

*Abstem.* And yet there are many students here who make not altogether unsatisfactory progress.

*Glauc.* Yes. Little boys are led by their parents to the schools as to an operative shop, by which afterwards they can derive a living. The very teachers themselves, incredible to say, as little as the pupils, cherish the occupation they follow with such slight honour and with such meagre reward, so that illustrious teachers of the first rank can scarcely maintain themselves.

*Asot.* This has nothing to do with the subject of our conversation. Let us return to the banquet.

*Glauc.* Yes, I would rather hear about that, but dismiss this talk about studies, which are certainly unfruitful. I know not how you Italians think about scholarship. In my eyes, it seems to me not only useless but even pernicious (*damnosa*).

*Abstem.* So it seems to an ox and a pig, as it does to you. We, too, should think the same if we had not more intelligence than you.

## II. *The Exposition (Narratio)*

*Asot.* If we let you go on, there would be no end.

Therefore, listen. First, we all of us reclined, severe and serious. Grace was said, and everywhere was silence and quiet. Every one began to get his knife ready. We put on the appearance not of eagerness but of restraint (*non invitatorum sed invitorum*), so that you would have said that we were compelled to eat, and in the act of eating, did it as if reluctantly, for our mind had not as yet warmed with the ardour of spontaneity. Each one placed his napkin over his shoulders; some indeed in front of their chests. Others spread the tablecloth over their knees. One takes bread, looks at it, cleans it, if there is any coal or cinders lining it. All these things are done gently and lingeringly (*cunctabunde*).

### Cause

Some began the meal by drinking; others, before they drank, took a little salad and salted beef to arouse their sleeping appetite and to stimulate their languor. The first cup was of beer, so that there might be a cold, firm foundation underlaid for the warmth of wine. Then that holy liquor was brought first in narrow and small cups, which should rather irritate than assuage thirst. The host was a very festive man, than whom there was none better in the whole neighbourhood, nor even his equal, *i.e.*, in my opinion (which may be said without injury to any one). He then orders the largest

of cups to be brought and a beginning was
made of drinking liberally, after the Greek
fashion, as a certain Philo-Greek said, who
once had studied at Lyons. Then we began
to talk, and then to get warm. Everywhere
joviality and laughing became general. Oh,
feasts and nights of the gods! We drank to
one another's health, and returned like for
like, with great equity. It would have been
unjust to gain a point over one's companion,
especially at such a time.

*Abstem.* Rightly, if it were merely a question of a chalice
of wine, but it is one's senses and intellect
which are in question, the chief possessions of
man. But if we are to talk over so copious
and festive a subject, first I must ask of you
whether you are drunk?

*Asot.* No, certainly not. This you can easily and truly
see from the connectedness of my talk. Do
you think, if I were drunk, that I could relate
all this in such an orderly fashion?

*Abstem.* Then it is well, for otherwise I should be con-
tending with an absent opponent, according to
the verse of Mimus. But tell me now, first,
why don't you erect a temple in these parts
to Bacchus, the discoverer of this celestial
liquor?

*Asot.* This is your business; you, who have a temple at
Rome of Sergius and Bacchus. It is sufficient
for us daily to follow his rites, wherever we are.
And perchance we should erect a temple for
him if it were settled he was the discoverer,

for I have heard certain students debate the question. There are some who think that Noah was the first who drank wine and was intoxicated by it.

*Abstem.* Let us leave that point! Tell us what wine you had.

*Asot.* What concerns us is what sort of wine it is and whence it came. Let it only have the name and colour of wine, that is sufficient for us. For these delicacies in wines let the Frenchman and the Italian seek.

*Abstem.* What enjoyment can there then be if you don't at all taste what you are pouring into your body?

*Tric.* Perchance some taste something at the beginning with the palate whole. But when it becomes palled from so great a superfluity, things lose all their taste.

*Abstem.* If thirst has been quenched, no pleasure remains. For this consists only in the satisfaction of natural needs. So it is a kind of torment to go on drinking when there is no thirst, or to eat when there is no hunger.

*Tric.* Don't you think, then, Abstemius, that we drink for pleasure or because it is pleasant?

*Abstem.* Then you are so much worse than beasts, who are controlled by natural desires, whilst reason does not govern you, nor nature exercise a control over you.

*Tric.* Good fellowship leads us to that point; and in spite of reason we get drunk little by little.

*Abstem.* How often have you been drunk? how often do you see others drunk?

*Tric.* Every day, very many.

*Abstem.* Don't then so many experiments satisfy you so as to put you on your guard against so disgraceful an event? Even one such experience would suffice for an animal!

*Glauc.* But do you know also how dear our companions are, for whose sake men become beasts? Whilst drinking they would give their very hearts for them. When they meet afterwards, they hardly know them! Their very life and soul they would not redeem for the sum of a sesterce.

*Abstem.* Out of what sort of cups and how did you quaff the wine?

*Asot.* In the first place there were brought glass cups; a little time afterwards, on account of the danger, these were taken away and silver ones presented. In the wine at first we put herbs, which the season of the year provided, a little time afterwards, flesh-broth, milk, butter, and pap.

*Abstem.* Oh, filth, which would not be borne by animals!

*Tric.* How much more tragically (τραγικώτερον) you would call out if you knew that they plunged their dirty hands into one another's wine and cast in the shells of eggs, fruit and nuts, and the stones of olives and prunes.

*Abstem.* Cease from this description, if you don't wish me to take myself off hence to some woods.

*Tric.* Listen to me, Glaucia. I will speak in your ear.

Some people carry a hunting-bugle when taking a journey, which is full of dust, straws, fluff, and other dirty things. Out of this we drank.

*Glauc.* What?

*Tric.* What, indeed? wine?

*Glauc.* Nay, rather say your understanding.

*Tric.* Clearly it is so. And after we had drunk the understanding we took pots (*matuli*), not altogether clean, from off a stool and used them for cups.

### Effects

*Abstem.* How ended the banquet—the story of which sounds like a fable?

*Asot.* The floors swam with wine. We were all drunk, especially the host, a strong man. Two or three were lying down under the table, overcome by a great victory.

*Abstem.* O glorious victory, and in a very beautiful and glorious conflict! But did wine overcome every one?

*Asot.* Even so.

*Abstem.* Wretched man, what do you think drunkenness is?

*Asot.* A fine thing! It is to give oneself up to one's genius.

*Abstem.* Yes, but which genius, your good one or your bad one?

*Glauc.* If you will rightly look into all these matters, you will never find which genius they give themselves up to. For it is neither to the heart, nor to pleasure, nor any other cause for which others indulge, who follow vices and the depraved desires of the mind. To be drunk is different. It is to lose the power of the senses, to go away from the power of reasoning, of judgment; clearly, from being a man to become either cattle or, indeed, a stone. What follows afterwards I can easily imagine, had I never seen a drunkard; to speak, and not to know what you are saying; if any secret, of especial importance not to be divulged, is committed to you, to blab it out, and to say things which may lead into grave danger yourself, your people, and often your whole province and fatherland, to have no discrimination of friend and foe, of wife and mother—and it leads to quarrels, contentions, enmities, snares, wounds, maiming, killing!

*Tric.* Even without sword and blood, for not a few pass on from drunkenness to death.

*Glauc.* Who would not prefer to be shut up at home with a dog or a cat than with a drunkard? For those animals have more intellect in them than the drunkard.

*Abstem.* After the drunkenness follows indigestion, weakening of the nerves, paralysis, the tortures of gout, heaviness in the head and the whole body, dulness of all the senses; memory is extinguished; the sharpness of the intellect is stunned; thence there is a stupor in the whole mind which precludes intelligence, wisdom, and eloquence.

*Asot.* Now I begin to understand what a serious evil drunkenness is; henceforward, I will take the keenest pains to drink up to the point of cheerfulness, not to that of drunkenness.

*Glauc.* Joviality is the gate of drunkenness. No one comes to be drunk with the idea in his mind that he will get drunk; but he is exhilarated by drinking; then going on and on, drunkenness follows afterwards, for it is difficult to place the bounds of joviality and to remain in it. Slippery is the step from joviality to drunkenness!

*Abstem.* So long as thou hast the wine in the beaker, it is in thy power; when thou hast it in thy body, thou art in the power of the wine. Then you are held and do not hold. When you drink, you treat wine as you like. When you have drunk, it will treat you as it likes.

*Asot.* What then? Are we never to drink?

*Abstem.* When fools avoid their vices, they run into the opposite extremes. We must, indeed, quench thirst, but not be " drinkers." Nature on this point teaches beasts alone. The same nature will not teach man, because he possesses reason. You eat when you are hungry; you drink when you are thirsty. Hunger and thirst will warn you how much, when, to what extent, we must eat and drink.

*Asot.* What if I am always thirsty, and if I cannot assuage my thirst except by getting drunk?

*Abstem.* Then drink what cannot possibly make you drunk.

*Asot.* The constitution of my body won't permit that.

*Abstem.* If then you had such hunger that by no amount of food you could satisfy it unless you were to burst yourself, what then?

*Asot.* That indeed would not be hunger, but disease.

*Abstem.* There would surely be need of medicine, not meals, to take away that hunger, wouldn't there?

*Asot.* Certainly.

*Abstem.* So needest thou for such a thirst a physician, not an inn-keeper, and a drug from the chemist, not one fetched from the providers of banquets. What you describe is not thirst but disease, and a perilous one, too!

# XIX

## REGIA—*The King's Palace*

AGRIUS, SOPHRONIUS, HOLOCOLAX

In this dialogue, the Royal Dwelling or Palace and its parts, persons, and functions are described, as to which see Vincentius Lupanus, in his book *de Magistratibus Francorum*. For our Vives here chiefly describes the palace of a French king. The persons represented in the dialogue are fitly named from the Greek. For Agrius is with them a country rustic, unskilled in court-life. Sophronius is a prudent, modest, and cautious man. Holocolax is altogether a flatterer, and one who (as Terence says) has commanded himself to agree to everything, of which sort of men there is always so large an assembly in courts. There are two parts of the dialogue, the Exordium and Narratio.

### I. *Introduction (Exordium)*

*Agri.* Why is it so many accompany the king in such varied styles of dress?

*Soph.* Nay, rather look on their countenances than on their finery. For their faces are more varied and diverse than their decorations and clothes.

*Agri.* What reason is there for this difference also of bearing?

### *Apparel—The Countenance*

*Soph.* They are clothed differently according to their means; differently according to their rank or family, often even according to their ambitions or vanity. Many also use elegancy of

163

dress as an angle and net for catching the favour of the king or of his chief officers, and, not rarely, for winning the maids of his court. But the expression of outward countenance follows the stirrings of the mind, and such outward expression is nearly always such as is prompted by the inner disposition of the mind.

*Agri.* But why do so many men meet here together?

*Holo.* Is it not fitting that very many people should come where the capital and government of the whole province are seated?

*Soph.* Quite so.   But most people regard not so much the commonwealth as their private good. They follow the government, not because it has the country in its hand, but because it has fortunes to bestow.

*Holo.* Why not?   Since all things are sold for money.

*Soph.* So they think who don't possess any soul and mind, but whose health and gifts of body are only common.

*Agri.* What need is there in this tumult of the court to hold so great a philosophical speculation?   I indeed should prefer to understand from you what sort of people these are in such great numbers, in such varied appearances and fashions.

*Holo.* I will tell you of them all, in their rank.   For Sophronius, as far as I know, is not so well versed in royal matters.   But I have been in royal company of all kinds; I have penetrated, inspected, and seen thoroughly their courts, and I have always been acceptable and pleasing to them all.

*Soph.* Thence I suppose it is that you have gained that name of yours, Holocolax.

## II. *Exposition* (*Narratio*)—*The King*

*Holo.* You suppose rightly. But do you, Agrius, listen to me. He yonder, on whom every ear, eye, mind, is intent, is the king, the head of the kingdom.

*Soph.* Truly the head, and so the health when he is wise and honest, but the ruin when he is bad or rash (*demens*).

### *The Dauphin—Dignitaries—Prefects*

*Holo.* The little boy who follows him is his son, his heir, whom in the Greek court they called despot, that is, lord (*dominus*). In Spain they call him prince, in France the dauphin. There with a neck-chain, like that of Torquatus, in clothes all of silk, or all of gold, are the leaders of the kingdom, with the decorations of names of military dignitaries, princes, dukes, lords of the marches, who are called *marchiones*, counts, men who are named barbarously, barons, knights. This one is the master of the horse, whom they call by the vulgar term of *comes stabilis*, a name taken from the Greek court, when the great Comestabulus (Constable) was, as it were, the prefect of the sea, the admiral. Further, he was supreme over the palace, and also was at the head of the guards. In the time of Romulus they named such an one *praefectus celerum*, and the guards themselves *celeres*.

*Agri.* Who are those in robes reaching to the ankles, and with faces of great severity?

### Counsellors

*Holo.* They are the counsellors of the king.

*Soph.* Those whom the prince calls to his council. It behoves them to be the most prudent of men, of great experience, of the greatest weight and moderation in their discernment.

*Agri.* Why so?

*Soph.* Because they are the eyes and ears of the prince, and so of the whole kingdom, and so much the more if the king should be blind or deaf, enslaved by his senses, or by ignorance, or by enjoyment of pleasure.

*Agri.* Are that one-eyed man and that other deaf man eyes and ears of the king?

*Soph.* Worse still is blindness and deafness of the heart!

### Secretaries

*Holo.* The secretaries follow the counsellors, nor are they few in number or of one rank; then those who deal in money matters for the king, or those who get it in, farmers of the taxes, treasury-tribunes, prefects, procurators, and advocates of the treasury.

*Agri.* Who are those luxuriously decked and festive young men who always follow the king and stand at his side, some laughing at him and

others with open mouth, full of wonder at
what he says?

*Courtiers*

*Holo.* These are a band of intimate friends, the delight
and joy of the king.

*Agri.* Why are the two who are entering there followed
by so many men full of grimaces?

*Chancellor—Secretary—Litigants—Prefect of the
Bed-chamber*

*Holo.* Because the king has in them especial confidence.
The one is the prefect of the sacred writings,
or chief secretary; the other the keeper of
the secret archives, amongst which are the
official statistics (*regni breviarium*). He has
to remind the king of everything. Therefore
daily so many come to him, so that they may
rub up and renew his memory, since that is the
keeping of the memory of the prince. Those
who draw in their countenances are litigants,
who are prosecuting their suits. Their business never finds an end, through the long series
of procrastinations which are kept up. Those
two who keep walking up and down the hall
are prefects, the one of the sleeping-chamber,
the other of the royal stables. These have
under them very many other chamber and
stable attendants. But let us enter the royal
dining-hall.

*Agri.* Ah, how great a crowd solicitous and stately in
their pomp!

*Soph.* You would observe these with still greater amaze-
ment if you knew how small a matter they are
attending to.   It is, forsooth, this: it is how a
sick man may suck up a single egg and drink
a little wine.

### Master of the Feast

*Holo.* That man is the master of the feast for this week.
There he is with an Indian who has a plait of
rushes on him.   That young man is the cup-
bearer.   The carver has not yet entered.

*Agri.* Who are about to have their breakfast (*pransuri*)
with the king?

*Holo.* You mean who is so lucky as to take part in this
feast of the gods?

*Soph.* Formerly guests were invited to the royal table,
sometimes experienced military commanders,
sometimes men of high lineage, or sometimes
those distinguished either by experience in
affairs, or by their learning, by whose discourse
the king would become better and wiser.   But
the pride of Goths and other barbarians has
invaded this our custom.

*Holo.* The chief followers have their grown-up armour-
bearers and their boy-followers, boys on foot
and spurred boys.   Amongst these are quite
magnificent, rich people, who most of them
take their meals in correct fashion, or if this
seems to them wearisome, they send basketfuls
to their friends.   This latter custom is more
useful to their poorer friends.   But the correct
fashion of feasting has more distinction in it.

*Agri.* I seem to see quite another sort of people in that eating-chamber.

### Ladies' Quarters

*Holo.* Those are the ladies' quarters, where the queen lives with her matrons and girls. Look how they enter and go out from the hall (*ex parthenone*) like as bees from a hive—young lovers and slaves of Cupid!

*Soph.* Often old people have a second childhood.

*Holo.* There is no greater pleasure than to hear the keenly thought-out sayings, or poems, songs, early morning (*antelucanus*) melodies, and chat of these girls, to see their briskness, their walking in and out, varieties of colour in their dress, their clothing and shapes of garments. They have boys as amanuenses, through whom they send and return messages. With what zeal and what industry, what breeding, they announce and bring back messages, hither and thither. By the faith of the gods! with uncovered heads, with bent hams and bowed knees. Every day there is something new to be heard, seen, and pondered over; something which has been acutely or subtly thought out or said, or done with spirit, or dexterously, or without restraint.

*Soph.* Nay, rather in a négligé way.

*Holo.* What greater happiness? Who could tear himself away from such delight?

*Soph.* Colax, Colax, without being in love you are raving, and without wine, you are drunk.

What foolishness could be greater than what
has been described by you?

*Holo.* I don't know how it happens that you see heaps
of people depart from the schools quite young,
but let them once enter the court, they become
old in it.

*Soph.* So also those who drank from the cup of Circe
would be unwilling to yield and return to their
human nature and condition, having once lost
their reason, and having degenerated into the
nature of beasts!

*Agri.* But what do all these do when they go home, and
with what actions do they occupy themselves
to pass the time, at least?

### Leisure Time—Flattery

*Soph.* The most of them do nothing more serious than
what you now observe them doing, and then
their leisure is for them the parent and nurse
of many vices. Some play at dice, cards, the
gaming-board, at disputations; others pass
the afternoon hours in secret slander and artful
calumny, that is to what they degenerate at
home. Many also are wonderfully taken up
with buffoons and jugglers, towards whom
those who are at other times niggardly and
sordid, to them they are most lavish. But
the chief corruption of the court is the flattery
of each to all the others, and, what is still worse,
towards himself. This brings it about that
no one ever hears salutary truths either from
himself nor from his companions unless when

at strife. And though he receives then all too
little of truth, he takes it as insult.

*Holo.* This employment is now by far the most profitable.
*You* may hunger and thirst after the love of
speaking and truth. *I* have become rich by
my smiling, blandishments, and by approving
and praising everything.

*Agri.* Could not the kings alter these unsatisfactory
matters?

*Soph.* Very easily, if they only wished to do so! But
these fashions are pleasing; they are similar
to their own. Others are precluded by their
preoccupations, on account of which they
never have leisure for doing anything which
is right or thinking anything which is sane.
There are also not lacking those who, with
indulgent minds and careless themselves, don't
think the morality of their own homes, and
that of their dependants, any concern of theirs.
And those things trouble them less than the
private home of each of us troubles any of us.

# XX

## PRINCEPS PUER—*The Young Prince*

MOROBULUS, PHILIPPUS, SOPHOBULUS

This dialogue is entirely " political," for Vives lays down the precepts to the boy prince, and teaches the art of good government. The names are aptly bestowed. Morobulus is a foolish counsellor, ἀ μωρὸς, foolish, βουλή, counsel; Sophobulus, a prudent counsellor. There are two parts of the dialogue.

### INSTITUTIO

| | |
|---|---|
| *Morobuli de* | { Inutilitate studiorum<br>{ Praeceptoribus |

| | | | |
|---|---|---|---|
| *Sophobuli de arte gubernandi* | ⌠ Quod principi sit necessaria: idque ostendit<br>⎮ tribus similitudinibus<br>⎮<br>⎨ Quomodo comparan- da sit | ⌠ Doctrina: ubi<br>⎮ ostendit, quinam<br>⎨ Consulendi<br>⎩ Ocii fuga | ⌠ Sine<br>⎮<br>⎨ Non<br>⎩ sint |

## I. *The Teaching of Morobulus—The Study of Literature*

*Morob.* What has your highness in hand, Philip?

*Phil.* I read and learn with zeal, as you can see for yourself.

*Morob.* I see only too well, and am pained that you weary yourself, and that you are making that little body of yours quite lean!

*Phil.* What then should I do?

*Morob.* That which other nobles, princes, and rich men

do—ride about, chat with the daughters of
your august mother, dance, learn the art of
bearing arms, play cards or ball, leap and run.
Such, you see, are the studies in which young
nobles most delight. If now people, who
scarcely are worthy to be received in your
family, enjoy these pleasant occupations, why
is it suitable for you to do as you are doing,
when you are the son and heir of so great a
prince?

*Phil.* What! is the study of letters no good?

*Morob.* It is indeed of good, but rather for those who
are initiated in holy affairs, *i.e.*, priests, or for
those who, by useful knowledge of their art,
are about to earn their living, such as the shoe-
maker's art, the weaving art, and the other arts
necessary for money-making. Rise, I beg of
you, put away your books from your hands.
Let us go out for a walk, so that for some short
time you may get fresh air!

*Phil.* I may not do so just now, because of Stunica and
Siliceus.

*Morob.* Who are these Stunica and Siliceus? Are they
not your subjects, over whom you have the
command, not they over you?

### Teachers

*Phil.* Stunica is my educator, while Siliceus is my
literary tutor. Subjects of mine indeed they
are, or to speak more exactly, of my father;
but my father, to whom I am subject, placed
them over me, and subjected me to them.

*Morob.* What then! Did your father give your highness into servitude to these men?

*Phil.* I don't know.

*Morob.* Oh! most unworthy deed!

## II. *The Teaching of Sophobulus*

*Soph.* By no means, my son! Certainly he made them thy servants; he wished them to stick close to thee, as eyes, ears, soul, and mind, to be always engaged on thy behalf, each of them to put aside his own affairs, and to make thy affairs his sole business, not so as to vex thee by imperiousness; but that those good and wise men should transform thy uncultivated manners into the virtue, glory, and excellence of a man; not so as to make thee a slave, but truly a free man and truly a prince. If thou dost not obey them, then wilt thou be a slave of the lowest order, worse than those here amongst us who are employed, bought and sold from Ethiopia or Africa.

*Morob.* Whose slave, then, would he be, if he did not mould his morals after his educators?

*Soph.* Not of men certainly, but of vices, which are more importunate masters, and more intolerable than a dishonest and wicked man!

*Phil.* I don't quite understand what you say.

*Soph.* But did you understand Morobulus?

*Phil.* Most clearly, everything.

*Soph.* Oh, how happy men would be, if they had the sense and intelligence for good and satisfactory things which they have for frivolous and bad

things! Now indeed, on the contrary, at your
time of life, it happens that you understand with ease what is trifling, what is
inept, nay, even what is insane, such things as
those to which Morobulus has exhorted you,
and then you regard what I would say on
virtue, dignity, and every kind of praiseworthy
thing, as if I were speaking Arabic or Gothic.

*Phil.* What, then, are you of opinion I ought to do?

*Soph.* You should at least suspend your judgment.
Neither acquiesce in the opinions of Morobulus, nor in mine, until you are able to judge
as to both.

### The Act of Governing

*Phil.* Who will give me this power of judgment?

*Soph.* Ah! that will come with age, teaching, and
experience.

*Morob.* Alas! that would require long weariness of
waiting!

### First Similitude

*Soph.* Morobulus advises well. Throw away your
books. Let us go and play! Let us play a
game in which one is elected king. He will
prescribe to the others what should be done.
The rest obey, according to the laws of the
game. You shall be king.

*Phil.* How shall the game be? For if I don't know the
game, how shall I be able to take the part of
king in it?

### Second Similitude

*Soph.* What are you saying, sweetest little Philip, the
darling of Spain? You would not dare to
undertake to rule in a game, not knowing it,
in a game and frivolous matters, in which a
mistake brings no particular danger; and you
are willing seriously to undertake to rule so
many and so great kingdoms, ignorant of the
condition of the people and of the laws of
administration, although uninstructed in all
prudence, and only knowing the ridiculous
trivialities, which Morobulus here instils in
your mind? Ah! my boy, tell the Master of
the Horse to lead forth hither that Neapolitan
horse, the most ferocious kicker, and the one
given to throw his rider to the ground, and let
Philip ride him!

*Phil.* By no means that one, but another and safer one.
For I have not as yet learned the art of managing a refractory horse, and I have not the
strength for it!

### Third Similitude

*Soph.* Well, Philip, let me ask you whether you think
that a lion is equally fierce as a horse; or that
a horse will kick and be refractory, and less
obedient to the bridle than people, and the
host of men in a country who come together
and congregate from every kind of vice,
passion, crime, and evil deed; from agitations
which have been fanned so as to be incensed,

inflamed, burning into flame? You would not
dare to mount a horse, while you demand that
you should rule over a people, more difficult
still to govern and manage than any horse!
But let us dismiss this illustration. Do you
see that boat on the river? The navigation
is most pleasant and delightful between the
meadows and the willow-plantings. Come,
let us go down to it. You shall sit at the
rudder and guide the boat.

*Phil.* Yes, indeed! and overturn you and plunge you
into the water, as Pimentellulus lately did!

*Soph.* What! you are not willing to guide a boat, on a
stream so even and so calm, because untrained,
and yet you will commit yourself to that sea,
to those waves and tides, to that tempest of
the people, without knowledge and without
experience? Evidently it has befallen you
as it did Phaethon, who was ignorant of the
art of charioteering, and yet, with youthful
ardour, he requested that he might take the
management of his father's chariot! I think
that story is known to you. Isocrates used to
say excellently, that the two greatest offices in
the life of men were those of the prince and the
priest. No one, he said, should seek after
them, unless he were worthy. No one should
believe himself able rightly to rule, unless he
were the most prudent man in the kingdom.

*Phil.* I see that nothing is so necessary for my person
and station as the knowledge of the art and
skill of ruling a kingdom.

*Soph.* Evidently you grasp the matter.

*Phil.* How can I pursue my duty?

### How the Art of Governing is to be Acquired

*Soph.* Hast thou received the knowledge of governing at thy birth?

*Phil.* Indeed, no!

*Soph.* By what means, then, canst thou get to know except by learning?

*Phil.* There is no other way.

*Soph.* With what countenance, then, can Morobulus advise you, that you should throw away your studies, by which you may obtain experience in your art, as well as knowledge of other subjects of the greatest and most attractive kind?

*Phil.* From whom, then, can knowledge of these subjects be obtained?

*Soph.* From those who have reflected on them, and observed them as they have been manifested in the greatest minds, of whom some are dead, others living.

*Phil.* But how can we learn from the dead? Can the dead speak?

*Soph.* Have you never in conversation heard the names of Plato, Aristotle, Cicero, Seneca, Livy, Plutarch?

### 1. Teachers no longer Living

*Phil.* These are great names! I have heard them spoken of often, and with great admiration and praise.

*Soph.* These very names and many others like them,

already departed from this life, will talk with
you as often and as much as you like.

*Phil.* How?

*Soph.* In books, which they have left behind for the
benefit of posterity.

*Phil.* How is it that these are not already in my hand?

*Soph.* They shall be given to you soon, after you have
learned that language, in which you will be
able to understand what they say.   Only wait
a little, and go through with the short burden
which must be endured in receiving the elementary basis of instruction;  after that follow
incredible delights.   It is no wonder that without such a preparation the idea of literary
studies is abhorrent.   But those who have
enjoyed them would sooner be plucked from
life itself than be torn away from books and
intellectual interests.

## 2. *Living Teachers*

*Phil.* But pray tell me, who are those living people
from whom this wisdom and soundness of
mind can be learned?

*Soph.* If you were about to undertake any journey,
from whom would you earnestly inquire the
road?   Would it be from those who had never
seen the road, or from those who had at some
time accomplished the journey?

*Phil.* From those, forsooth, who had travelled on that
journey!

*Soph.* Is not this life even as a journey, and is it not a
perpetual starting out?

*Phil.* So it seems.

*Soph.* Who, therefore, have performed this journey the most thoroughly? Old men or youths?

*Phil.* Old men.

*Soph.* Old men, then, should be consulted.

*Phil.* All indifferently?

*Soph.* That is an acute question; not all promiscuously. But in the same manner as it is with the journey, so it is with life. Do those know the way of life, who have gone along it without reflecting on it, busying themselves with something else, their minds wandering no less than their body; or those who have noted things diligently and attended to them, one by one, and committed what they have observed to their memory?

*Phil.* To be sure it is the latter.

*Soph.* Therefore, in taking counsel concerning the method of leading our life, it is not young men to whom we should listen, for they have not been over the journey, much less youths, and, what is most foolish and inappropriate, boys. Nor is counsel to be sought from foolish, lascivious, demented old men, worse than boys, whom the divine oracles execrate, because they are boys of a hundred years of age. Ears should be open to old men of great judgment, experienced in things, and prudent in mind.

*Phil.* By what sign shall I know them?

*Soph.* To be sure, at thy age, my son, thou canst not as yet distinguish them by any sign; but when a

greater and stronger judgment has developed
in thee, thou wilt easily recognise them by their
words and deeds, as affording the clearest of
signs. In the meantime, whilst thou hast not
strength in this power of judgment, trust thyself entirely, and commit the direction, to thy
father, and to those whom thy father has
appointed as instructors and teachers and
governors of thy early years—those who, as
it were, lead thee by the hand, along that road
on which thou hast not yet journeyed. For
there is a greater care over thee exercised by
thy father (to whom thou art dearer than he is
to thee) than thou couldst have for thyself,
and, in this matter, not only has he his own
experience to guide him, but he makes use of
the counsel of wise men.

*Morob.* For too long I have been silent.

*Soph.* Quite so, though contrary to your custom. For
some time I have felt keen astonishment at
the fact.


### The Sort of Leisure to be Shunned—The Assertion of the Similitude (Protasis)

*Morob.* Philip, do not your father and the King of France
and other great kings and princes rule their
kingdoms and territories, and hold them in
their duty, without the study of letters, and
without that burdensome labour, which here is
imposed mercilessly on your tender shoulders?

*Soph.* Nothing is so easy that it cannot become difficult,

if it is done unwillingly. Industrious labour,
devoted to learning, is not wearisome to him
who gives his attention to it gladly. But to
him who is unwilling, if indeed it is a game
that is in question, or if it were a case of taking
a walk in the most pleasant spots, it is troublesome and intolerable. To thee, Morobulus,
most eager for trifling and always accustomed
to frivolity, either to do anything serious or
even to hear of it, is as unpleasant as death.
Certainly many others would regard their life
as bitter, if the manner of their living were
fixed according to the fashion of Morobulus.
How many there are, especially in courts, to
whom nothing is sweeter than a sluggish and
inert leisure! To move their hands to do work
is to put them on the torture-rack! How
many there are, on the other hand, amongst
the people, who would die rather than pass
through all their days with such vacuity, and
would get weary more quickly by doing nothing
than by giving their closest attention to some
business! But to answer you concerning the
Emperor and King of France, you shall hear
from me about old men in general, whom I take
to be those who have run over the track of life.
If all, whosoever have made the journey, with
unanimity say that they have fallen on some spot
full of difficulty and danger, from which place
they have only got away wounded and broken
down to the last degree; but if they had that
journey to go over again they would take care

for nothing more diligently than against that
danger. What do you think, would it not be
the part of a most foolish man, when he had to
take that way again, not to recall the danger
and not to know it was coming?

*Phil.* Not as yet do I grasp what you mean!

*Soph.* I will make it more clear by an example.
Imagine that, over the river yonder, there was
a narrow plank as bridge, and that every one
told you that as many as rode on horseback
and attempted thus to cross it, had fallen into
the water, and were in danger of their lives,
and, moreover, that with difficulty they had
been dragged out half-dead. Do you understand this?

*Phil.* Most clearly.

*Soph.* Would not, in such a case, a man seem to you to
be demented who, taking that journey, did
not get off from his horse, and escape from the
danger in which the others had fallen?

*Phil.* To be sure he would.

### Its Explanation (Apodosis)

*Soph.* And rightly! Seek now from old men, as to what
chiefly they have felt unfortunate in this life,
what it grieves them most and what they
bitterly regret to have neglected. All will
answer with one voice, so far as they have
learned anything, it is, not to have learned more.
So far as they have not learned, they will regret
that they did not take pains to acquire the
knowledge. Having entered on this complaint

against themselves, they will tell you over and
over again, that their parents or educators sent
them to schools and to teachers of literature,
yet that they, drawn on by vain delights,
either of play, or hunting, or love, or frivolity
of some kind, let drop from their hands the
opportunities of learning; and so they complain of their fate and bewail their lot, and
accuse themselves, condemn themselves, and, at
times, also curse themselves. You see now the
state of slackness and ignorance on the road
of life is especially unsafe and dangerous, and
is the one chiefly to be avoided, since you
hear the miserable cries of those who have
fallen there. It is therefore to be avoided
with all care and diligence. It is incumbent
on youth, to reject and despise sluggishness,
ease, little delicacies, and frivolity, whilst the
whole mind should be intent on the study of
letters and the cultivation of goodness of soul.
You, then, ask your father on this matter,
although he is yet a young man, and do you,
Morobulus, ask yours, although an old man,
and you will understand from them that my
opinion is the true one.

# XXI

## LUDUS CHARTARUM SEU FOLIORUM—
### Card-playing or Paper-games

Valdaura, Tamayus, Lupianus, Castellus,
Manricus

This Dialogue has two parts: Exordium and the game.
The Exordium is an introduction as to time (à *tempore*).

### I. *Introduction on the Weather*

*Val.* What rough weather! How cold and cruel the
heavens! how unfavourable the sun!

*Tam.* To what does this state of the heavens and the
sun point?

*Val.* That we should not go out of the house.

*Tam.* But what are we to do in the house?

*Val.* Study by the lighted hearth, meditate, think on
things—a course which might bring profit and
sound morals to the mind.

*Cast.* This is indeed the chief thing to be done, nor ought
anything to take precedence of it in a man's
mind. But when a man's mind is wearied by
intentness of application, how then shall he
divert himself, especially in such weather as
this?

*Val.* Some recreations of the mind suit some people;
others, others. I indeed receive delight and
recreation by card games.

*Tam.* And this kind of weather invites in that direction,

185

so that we hide ourselves in a closely shut
room, and guarded on every side from the
wind and cold, with a shining hearth, and a
table set with charts (*i.e.* maps).

*Val.* Alas! we have no charts.

*Tam.* I mean playing-cards.

*Val.* I should like that.

*Tam.* Then we want some money and stones (*calculi*)
for reckoning.

*Val.* We don't need stones, if we have some very small
coins.

*Tam.* I have none, except gold and larger silver coins.

*Val.* Change some for small money. Here, boy, take
these coins of one, two, two-and-a-half, and
three, stivers and get us tiny coins from the
money-changer—single, two, three, farthing-
pieces, not bigger money.

*Tam.* How these coins shine!

*Val.* Certainly, they are as yet new and unused.

*Tam.* Let us go to the games - emporium, where we
shall find everything ready to hand.

*Cast.* It is not expedient, for we should have such a
number of umpires. We might just as well
play in the public street. It would be better
to betake ourselves into your room, and invite
a few of our friends, especially those likely to
put us in good spirits.

*Tam.* Your chamber is more convenient for this, for in
mine, we should be interrupted continually by
the mother's maidservants, who are always
seeking some dirty clothes in the women's
chests.

*Val.* Let us go then into the dining-room.

*Tam.* So let it be. Let us go! Boy, fetch us here Franciscus Lupianus and Roderick Manricus and Zoilaster.

*Val.* Stay! By no means let us have Zoilaster, an angry man, given to quarrelling, a noisy calumniator, one who often raises fierce tragedies out of the smallest matters.

*Cast.* You certainly advise wisely, for if a young man of such views of recreation should mix himself in our company, then there would not be sport but grave strife. Bring, therefore, Rimosulus instead of him.

*Val.* No, not him, unless you wish whatever we do here, by way of sport, should be made known before sunset throughout the city.

*Cast.* Is he so good a herald?

*Val.* Yes, in making things known where no good is done by the knowledge. As to matters of good report, he is more religiously silent than the Eleusinian mysteries.

*Tam.* Then Lupianus and Manricus alone are to come.

*Cast.* They are first-rate companions.

*Tam.* And warn them to bring little coins with them, but whatsoever is of severity and earnestness let them leave at home with the crabbed Philoponus. Let them come, accompanied by jests, wit, and agreeableness.

*Lup.* Hail! most festive companions!

*Tam.* What is the meaning of that contraction of your brow? Smooth those wrinkles. Haven't you

been advised to lay down all thoughts of
literature in the abode of the Muses?

*Lup.* Our thoughts on literature are so illiterate that the
Muses who are in their abode wouldn't own
them.

*Manr.* All prosperity!

*Val.* Prosperity is doubtful, when you are called to the
line of battle and to warfare, in which, indeed,
kings will be present!

*Tam.* Be of good cheer! Money-purses, not necks, will
be attacked.

*Lup.* The money-purse often is in place of a neck, and
money in place of blood and spirit; as with
those Carians, whose contempt of life is the
pretext for kings to practise their madness on
them.

*Manr.* I don't wish to be an actor in, but the spectator
of, this play.

*Tam.* How so?

*Manr.* Because I am so very unfortunate; I always go
away from playing, beaten and despoiled.

*Tam.* Do you know what dice-players say, in a proverb
of theirs? " You should seek your toga
where you lost it."

*Manr.* True, but there is the danger that, while I seek
the lost toga, I shall lose both my tunic and
shirt.

*Tam.* This indeed often happens, but he who risks
nothing does not become rich.

*Manr.* This is the opinion of metal-diggers.

*Tam.* Also of the Janus in the middle of Antwerp.

## II. *The Playing—Drawing Lots*

*Val.* It is quite right.   We can only play four at a time.
We are five.   Let us cast lots as to who shall
be the spectator of the others.

*Manr.* I will be the one, without any casting of lots.

*Val.* No such thing!   Wrong should be done to none.
No one's will, but chance, shall decide this.
He to whom the first king falls in dealing, he
shall sit as lazy spectator, and if any dispute
shall arise, he shall be judge.

*Lup.* Here are two whole packs of cards; one is
Spanish, the other French.

*Val.* The Spanish does not seem to be quite right.

*Lup.* How so?

*Val.* Since the tens are lacking.

*Lup.* They don't usually have them, as the French do.
Cards, both Spanish and French, are divided
into four suits, or families.   The Spanish have
gold coins, cups, sceptres, and swords.   The
French, hearts, diamonds, clubs, (little) plough-
shares, otherwise called spades or arrow-points.
There are in each suit—king, queen, knight;
ones, twos, threes, fours, fives, sixes, sevens,
eights, nines.   The French also have tens.   In
the Spanish game, golden pieces and cups are
used, but less preferably swords and sceptres.
With the French, the higher numbers are
always considered better.

*Cast.* What game shall we play?

*Val.* The game of Spanish Triumph, in which the
dealer will retain for himself the last card

as indication (of trumps) if it is a one or a picture.

*Manr.* Let us know now who shall be left out of the game!

*Tam.* You advise well. Pray deal the cards. This is yours, this is his, this for Lupianus. You are umpire.

*Val.* I would rather have you as umpire than as a fellow-player.

*Lup.* Nice words, I must say. Pray, why do you say so?

*Val.* Because in playing you are so cunning, and such a caviller. Then they say that you have a knack of arranging the cards as suits yourself.

*Lup.* My play has no deceit in it. But my activity seems to your lack of experience like imposture, as often is the case with the ignorant. However, how does Castellus please you, who, as soon as he has won a little money, leaves off playing?

*Tam.* This is rather shirking play than playing itself (*eludere est hoc, quam ludere*).

*Val.* That is a light evil enough. For if he should be beaten, he will fasten himself to the game like a nail in a beam.

### Partners

*Tam.* We will play by twos, two against two. How shall we be partnered?

*Val.* I, indeed, knowing nothing of this game, will stick to you, Castellus, whom I understand to be most expert in the game.

*Tam.* Add also, most crafty in it.

*Cast.* There is no need of choosing. Lots must divide everything. Those who get the highest cards play against those with the lowest.

*Val.* So be it. Deal the cards!

*Manr.* As I wished, Castellus and I are on the same side. Valdaura and Tamayus are our opponents.

*Val.* Let us sit, as we are accustomed, crosswise.

Give me that reclining chair, so that I may lose more peacefully.

*Tam.* Place the footstool. Let us sit down in our places. Draw for the lead.

*Val.* It is my lead. You deal, Castellus.

### *Modes of Distribution of Cards*

*Cast.* How? from the left to the right, according to the Belgian custom? or, on the contrary, according to Spanish custom, from the right to the left?

*Val.* By the latter custom, since we are playing the Spanish game and have thrown out the tens.

*Cast.* Yes. How many cards do I give to each?

### *The Stake*

*Val.* Nine. But what shall the stake be?

*Manr.* Three denarii each deal and a doubling of the stakes

*Cast.* Wait, my Manricus, you are getting on too fast! That would not be play, but madness, where so much money would be risked. How could you have pleasure in the anxiety lest you should lose so much money? One denarius would be sufficient, and the increase shall be one-half up to five asses.

*Val.* You counsel rightly. For so we shall not play without stakes, which would be insipid, nor for what would grieve us, if we lost, for that is bitter.

*Cast.* Have you all nine cards? Hearts are trumps, and this queen is mine.

*Val.* What a happy omen that is! Certainly it is most true that the hearts of women ordinarily rule.

*Cast.* Leave off your reflections. Answer to this: I increase the stake!

### The Contest

*Val.* I have a losing hand and haven't good sequences. I pass.

*Tam.* And I also. You deal, Manricus.

*Val.* What are you doing? You haven't shown the trump.

*Manr.* I will first count my cards, so as not to have more or less than nine.

*Val.* You have one too many.

*Manr.* I will place one aside.

*Val.* That is not the rule of the game. You ought to lose your turn of dealing, and pass it on to the next. Give me the cards!

*Manr.* I won't, since I haven't yet turned up the trump.

*Val.* Yes, you will.  By God (*per Deum*)!

*Cast.* Get away!  What has come into your mind, my Valdaura?  You swear oaths on the slightest provocation, which would scarcely be fitting on the most important affairs.

*Manr.* What do you say, umpire?

*Lup.* I don't know really what should be done in this case.

*Manr.* See what a judge we have appointed over us—one who has no judgment—a leader without eyes.

*Val.* What, then, is to be done?

*Manr.* What, indeed, unless we send to Paris for some one to bring this matter of ours forward for a decree of the Senate.

*Cast.* Mix the cards, and deal again.

*Tam.* Oh! what a good hand I lose!  I shall not have another like it to-day!

*Cast.* Shuffle well those cards and deal them more carefully, one by one.

*Val.* Again, I increase the stakes.

*Tam.* Didn't I predict that I shouldn't have such a chance in my hands again to-day?  I am always most unfortunate.  Why do I so much as even look at a game?

*Cast.* This, indeed, is not playing.  It is afflicting ourselves.  Is it recreating ourselves and refreshing our minds, to get worried like this? Play ought to be play, not torment.

*Manr.* Be a little patient; don't throw your cards away.  You are getting into a panic!

*Val.* Then answer if you accept (the amount of the stake).

*Manr.* I accept, and increase it again.

*Val.* What! do you expect to put me to flight with your fierce words?   I don't pass.

*Manr.* Declare, once for all, and be quick about it. Do you agree?

*Val.* Yes, and with the greatest pleasure.  My mind prompts me to contest in such play for a still greater stake, but this will do amongst friends.

*Tam.* What! don't you count me amongst the living, so that you leave me out of consideration?

*Cast.* What, then, do you stake, you man of straw (*faenee*).

*Tam.* I, for my part, wish to increase the stake.

*Manr.* What do you say, Castellus?

*Cast.* At last you consult me, after you have increased the stake by your own arrangements.  I should not dare, on my hand, to stake up to such an increase.

*Val.* Give a definite answer.

*Cast.* I haven't the grounds for doing so.  Everything seems ambiguous and doubtful.  Hence I answer hesitatingly, timidly, diffidently.  Isn't this expressed sufficiently clearly?

*Manr.* Immortal God, what an abundance of words! The hail we lately had, did not fall so thickly! But, I beg, let us risk a little.

*Cast.* Let us make the attempt when you please, but don't expect a great stake from me.

*Manr.* But you will bring what assistance you can?

*Cast.* There is no need for you to advise me on that score.

*Manr.* We have been completely beaten!

*Tam.* We have won four denarii.  Shuffle!

*Val.* I go five asses.

*Cast.* I don't know whether I shall pass, for I am sure to be beaten.

*Tam.* Five more!

*Cast.* What do you reply to this call?

*Manr.* What am I to say?  I let it pass.

*Cast.* You lost the last game.  Let me lose this in accordance with my own ideas.  I know that I am of less skill, but I must hold out as long as I seem to have any strength.

*Val.* What, then, do you say?  Do you refuse?

*Cast.* No, certainly.  I agree.

*Tam.* Don't you know this Castellus, Valdaura?  He plays a better game than you, but he is thus accustomed to lure on rash challengers into his net.  Take care not to go on rashly, where you will be entangled in a net.

*Val.* God's faith! how could you guess that I had one last card left of this suit (*natio*)?

*Cast.* I knew all the cards.

*Val.* That is quite conceivable.

*Cast.* And that, too, without looking at them!

*Val.* Perhaps even from the backs?

*Cast.* You are too suspicious.

*Val.* You make me so, if you will excuse me saying so.

*Tam.* Let us examine if the backs of the cards have marks whereby they can be recognised.

### End of the Game

*Val.* Let us, please, make an end of playing.  This game worries me by all going so wrongly.

*Cast.* As you will. But perchance the fault is not in
the game, but in your lack of skill, for you
don't know how to direct your steps to victory,
but you throw away your cards without any
reason, as chance happens, thinking that it
doesn't matter what you have played before,
or might play later, what and in what place
any card should be played.

*Tam.* Of all things there is satiety, and even of
pleasures. I am now weary of sitting. Let us
get up for a little time.

*Lup.* Take this lute and sing something to us.

*Tam.* What will you have?

*Lup.* A song on games.

*Tam.* A song of Vergil's?

*Lup.* Yes; or if you prefer one of Vives, the song he
lately sang as he wandered along the wall-
promenade of Bruges.

*Val.* With the voice of a goose.

*Lup.* But you sing it with a swan's voice!

*Tam.* This a god would do better, for the swan only
sings as death urges him on.

> Ludunt et pueri, ludunt juvenesque senesque
> Ingenium, gravitas, cani, prudentia, ludus,
> Denique mortalis sola virtute remota,
> Quid nisi nugatrix, et vana est fabula, vita.[1]

*Val.* I can assure you the song is well expressed, though
it comes as it were from a dry old stick (*ex
spongia arida*).

---

[1] Boys play, and play, also, youth and age. Play is the wit,
seriousness, and wisdom of old age. Also human life, what is
it but trifling and empty fable, when virtue is not its sole guiding
principle?

*Lup.* Does he compose a song with such great difficulty?

*Val.* Indeed he does.  Whether it is because he writes poetry so rarely, or because he does not do it willingly, or because the inclination of his genius drives him into other regions.

# XXII

## LEGES LUDI—*Laws of Playing*

### A VARIED DIALOGUE ON THE CITY OF VALENCIA

#### BORGIA, SCINTILLA, CABANILLIUS

Valencia is a town of Spain, the native town of Vives. To it Ptolemaeus gives 14° longitude, 39° latitude. *See* the same in the fourth map, Europe. There is another Valencia in France, as to which *see* the fifth map of Europe. This dialogue contains, to a large extent, the description of the native town of Ludovicus Vives. There are two parts of the dialogue. In the former part he describes two cities: Paris with its games, and Valencia; in the latter part he prescribes the laws of play. Ammianus Marcellinus calls Paris (Lutetia) *Parisiorum castellum.* The Emperor Julianus in an oration with the title Αντιοχιὸs ἢ μισοπώγων [1] calls it των παρισίων την πολιχνὴν ; [2] where also he shows for what reason he once was driven at Lutetia to vomit his food, viz., when impatient of the French custom, by which they were accustomed to heat their rooms by means of stoves (*fornaces*). Coal having been taken to the sleeping-chamber of Vives, he was almost killed by the fumes. *See* Beatus Rhenanus, book 3, *rerum Germanicarum*, at the end; Aegydius Corrozetus, *de antiquitat. Parisiens.*; and Zuingerus, book 3, *methodi Apodemicae.*

### PART I. *Lutetia*

*Borg.* Whence comest thou, most delightful Scintilla?

*Scin.* From Lutetia.

*Borg.* What Lutetia is that?

*Scin.* Do you ask which Lutetia, as if there were many!

---

[1] Viz., *The Antiochian ; or, The Beard-hater.*
[2] *I.e.*, the small town of the Parisians.

*Borg.* If there is only one, I don't know what it is, or
where it is situated.

*Scin.* It is the Parisian Lutetia (*Lutetia Parisiorum*).

*Borg.* I have often heard the Parisians spoken of, but
never Lutetia. It is, then, that Lutetia which
we call Paris? This is the reason then why, for
so long, no one has seen thee at Valencia; and
especially hast thou been missed at the tennis
court (*sphaeristerium*) of the nobles.

*Scin.* I have seen at Lutetia other tennis courts, other
gymnasia, other games, far more useful and
more attractive than yours at Valencia.

*Borg.* What are those, pray?

*Scin.* There are thirty gymnasia, more or less, in that
university (*academia*), which provides for every
kind of erudition, knowledge, and wisdom;
learned teachers, and most studious youths,
who are thoroughly well-bred.

*Borg.* Forsooth, a crowd of people!

*Scin.* What do you call a crowd?

*Borg.* The dregs of the people, sons of shoemakers,
weavers, barbers, fullers, and every kind of
operative artificers.

*Scin.* I see that you people here measure the whole
world by your city, and think that all Europe
has the same customs which you have here. I
can tell you, that the youth there very largely
consists of princes, leaders of men, nobles, and
the wealthiest persons, not only from France,
but also from Germany, Italy, Great Britain,
Spain, Belgium, marvellously devoted to the
study of letters, obeying the precepts and in-

structions of their teachers. Their conduct
is not formed through simple admonition
merely, but by sharp reproof and, when it is
necessary, even by punishment, by blows and
lashes. All which they receive and bear with
modest mind and the most collected countenance.

### Valencia

*Caban.* I have often heard stories told of the university,
when I was acting as ambassador (*legatus*) of
King Ferdinand. But please now leave this
topic, or defer it for another time. You see
that we have now entered the Miracle Play-
ground (*in ludo Miraculi*), which lies next to
the Carrossi Square. Come, now, let our conversation turn to the pleasurable topic of the
playing-ball (*pila*).

*Scin.* I should like it as long as we don't sit down, but
go on talking, as we walk about. Then it
would be very agreeable. Where shall we go?
Shall we take this way, which leads to St.
Stephen's Church, or that way to the Royal
Gate, where we then can visit the palace of
Ferdinand, Duke of Calabria?

*Caban.* Don't let us by any chance interrupt the studies
in wisdom of that best of princes.

### Walk through the City of Valencia

*Borg.* It would be better if we were to get mules so that
we might ride and talk.

*Caban.* Don't let us, I beg, lose the use of the feet and the legs; the weather is clear and bright, and the air cool; it will be more satisfactory to go on foot than on horseback.

*Borg.* Then let us go this way by St. John's Hospital to the Marine Quarter.

*Caban.* Let us observe, by the way, the beautiful objects we pass by.

*Borg.* What, on foot! This will be a disgrace.

*Scin.* In my opinion, it is a greater disgrace if men hang upon the judgments of inexperienced and stupid girls.

*Caban.* Would you like to go straight along Fig Street and St. Thecla Street?

*Scin.* No, but through the quarter of the Cock Tavern *(tabernae gallinaceae)*. For in that quarter I should like to see the house in which my Vives was born. It is situated, as I have heard, to the left as we descend, quite at the end of the quarter. I will take the opportunity to call upon his sister.

*Borg.* Let us put aside calling on women, but if you wish to speak with a woman, let us go rather to Angela Zabata, with whom we could have a chat on questions of learning.

*Caban.* If you wish to do so, would that we met the Marchioness Zeneti!

*Scin.* If those reports, which I heard of her when I was in France, were true, then we might have a greater subject of discussion than could easily be treated especially by those busied about anything else.

*Borg.* Let us go up to St. Martin's or down through the
Vallesian Quarter to the Villa Rasa Street.

*Caban.* From that place to the tennis court (*sphaeristerium*) of Barzius, or, if you prefer, to that of
the Masconi.

### Games—Ball

*Borg.* Have you also in France, public grounds for games
like ours?

*Scin.* As to other French cities, I cannot answer you.   I
know that there is none in Paris, but there are
many private grounds, for example, in the
suburbs of St. James, St. Marcellus, and St.
Germanus.

*Caban.* And in the city itself the most famous, which is
called Braccha.

*Borg.* Is the game played in the same way as here?

*Scin.* Exactly so, except that the teacher there furnishes
playing shoes and caps.

*Borg.* What sort are they?

*Scin.* The shoes are made of felt.

*Borg.* But they would not be of any use here.

*Caban.* That is, on a stony road.   In France indeed,
and in Belgium, they play on a pavement,
covered over with tiles, level and smooth.

*Scin.* The caps worn are lighter in summer, but in
winter, thick and deep, with a band under the
chin, so that as the player moves about, the
cap shall not fall off the head or fall down over
the eyes.

*Borg.* We don't here use a band, except when there is a

pretty strong wind. But what kind of balls do they use?

*Scin.* Not such light wind-balls as here, but smaller balls than yours, and much harder, made of white leather. The stuffing of the balls is not, as it is in yours, wool torn from rags, but chiefly dogs' hair. For this reason the game is rarely played with the palm of the hand.

*Borg.* In what way, then, do they strike the ball? with the fist, as we do the leather ball?

*Scin.* No, but with a net.

*Borg.* Woven from thread?

*Scin.* From somewhat thicker strings, such as are found for the most part on the six-stringed lyre. They have a stretched rope, and, as to the rest, the game is played as in the houses here. To send the ball under the rope is a fault, or loss of a point. There are two signs or, if you prefer, limits. The counting goes fifteen, thirty, forty-five or (advantage), equality of numbers and victory, which is twofold, as when it is said: " We have won a game " or " We have won a set." The ball, indeed, is either sent back whilst in its flight or thrown back after the first bound. For on the second bound, the stroke is invalid, and a mark is made where the ball was struck.

*Borg.* Are there no other games there except tennis?

*Scin.* In the city as many or more than here, but amongst scholars, no other is permitted by the masters. But sometimes, secretly, they play at cards and dice, the little boys with the knuckle-bones (*tali*), the worse sort of boys with dice (*taxilli*). We have a teacher Anneus who used to allow card-playing at festival times (*obscoeno die*). For that and for games in general, he composed six laws written on a tablet which he hung in his bed-chamber.

*Borg.* If it is not burdensome, may I ask you to tell them to us, in the same way as you have told us of other matters.

*Scin.* But let us continue our walk, for I am possessed by an inconceivably keen desire to behold my country which I have not seen for so long a period.

*Borg.* Let us mount mules, so that we may move along pleasantly, as well as with more dignity.

*Scin.* I would not give a snap of the fingers for this dignity!

*Borg.* And I, if I may confess the truth, would not move my hand for it. Nor do I know why riding on mules seems to be more becoming for us.

*Caban.* This is rightly said; we are three, and in the narrow streets or concourse of men we should get parted from one another, whence our talk would necessarily be interrupted, or many remarks made by some one of us would not be thoroughly heard or understood by the others.

*Borg.* So let it be; let us proceed on foot. Enter through this narrow lane on to the Peg-narogii Street.

## The Market

*Scin.* Nothing could be better. Thence by the key-
smith's into the Sweetmeats Quarter (*vicum
dulciarium*), then into the fruit market.

*Borg.* Nay, rather the vegetable market.

*Scin.* The market is both. Those who prefer to eat
vegetables call it the vegetable market; those
who prefer fruit call it the fruit market. What
a spaciousness there is of the market, what a
multitude of sellers and of things exposed for
sale! What a smell of fruit, what variety,
cleanliness, and brightness! Gardens could
hardly be thought to contain fruit equal to
the supply of what is in this market. What
skill and diligence our inspector (*aedilis*) of
public property and his ministers show so that
no buyer shall be taken in by fraud. Is not
he who is riding about so much, Honoratus
Joannius?

*Caban.* I think not, for one of my boys, who met him
just now, left him retiring to his library. If he
knew that we were here together then he would
undoubtedly join us in our conversation and
would postpone his serious studies to our play.

*Borg.* Now at last describe the laws of play!

*Scin.* We will withdraw from this crowd by the Street
of the Holy Virgin the Redeemer, to the
Smoky street and to St. Augustine's, where
there are fewer people.

*Caban.* Let us not go down so far away from the main
body of the city. Let us rather ascend

through the street of Money-Purses to the
Hill, then to the Soldiers' Quarter and the
house of your family, Scintilla, whose walls
yet seem to me to mourn over that hero, Count
Olivanus!

*Borg.* Nay, they have now laid aside their grief, and
now rejoice in all seriousness that such a youth
has stepped into the place of so great an old
man.

*Scin.* Oh, how delightful it is to look into the Senate
House (*curia*) and the fourfold court of the
governor of the city (*praefectus urbis*), which by
now seems almost to have become the heritage
of your family, Cabanillius—one part of the
building for a civil, another for a criminal, court,
and this part for the three hundred solidi. What
buildings! what a glory of the city!

### Part II. *The Laws of Play—The First Law*

*Borg.* In no place could you more rightly enunciate
laws than in the *forum* and *curia*, so give them
forth here! For some other time there will be
a more fitting occasion of discoursing on the
praise and admiration which our city excites.

*Scin.* The first law treats of the time of recreation
(*quando ludendum*). Man is constituted for
serious affairs, not for frivolity and recreation.
But we are to resort to games for the refreshing
of our minds from serious pursuits. The time,
therefore, for recreation is when the mind or
body has become wearied. Nor should other-

wise relaxation be taken, than as we take our
sleep, food, drink, and the other means of
renewal and recuperation. Otherwise it is
deleterious, as is everything which takes place
unseasonably.

### The Second Law

The second law deals with the persons with
whom we are to take our recreation (*cum
quibus ludendum*). In the same way as when
you are about to take a journey, or to go to a
banquet, you look about diligently to see who
are to be your future boon companions or
fellow travellers, so in considering your recreation, you should reflect with whom you will
play, so that they may be men known to you.
For there is a great danger with the unknown,
and it is a true proverb of Plautus: " A fellow-
man is a wolf to a man who does not know what
manner of associate he has got." Companions
should be agreeable, festive, with whom there
is no danger of quarrelling or fighting, of either
doing or saying anything disgraceful or un-
becoming! Let them not be blasphemers of
God, or users of oaths! Nor should they be
impure in speech, lest your morals should be
rubbed against by the contagion of what is
depraved or profligate. Lastly, they should
bring to the game no other purpose than your
own, viz., the idea of thorough rest from
labour, and the freedom from mental strain.

### The Third Law

The third law concerns the kind of recreation. First it should be a well-known game, for there can be no pleasure, if it is not known by player nor colleagues, nor by the lookers-on. Further, it must at the same time refresh the mind and exercise the body, if indeed the season of the year and state of health are suitable. But if not, it must be a game in which mere chance does not count for everything. There must be some skill in it, which may balance chance.

### The Fourth Law

The fourth law is as to stakes. You ought not to play so that the game is zestless, and quickly satiates you. So a stake may be justifiable. But it should not be a big one, which may disturb the mind in the very game itself, and if one is beaten, may vex and torture you. That is not a game; it is rather the rack.

### The Fifth Law

The fifth law treats of the manner of play, viz., that before you settle to play, you recall to mind that you have come for the invigoration of your mind, and for this object you may put a very small coin or two to stake, so as to purchase with them the recuperation from your weariness. Think that it is a chance, *i.e.*, variable, uncertain, unstable, common to all, and that no harm will be done to you through it, if you lose. Thus, you may have equanimity in your loss, so as not to contract your countenance and experience sadness over it—nor break forth into oaths and curses, either against your fellow-player, or any of the spectators. If you win, don't be insolently loquacious to your fellow-player! Be in all the game, his companion, cheerful, jovial, and mirthful, this side of scurrility and petulancy, nor must there be any trace of deceit, of sordidness or avarice. Don't be obstinate in contention and, least of all, make use of oaths —when you remember that the whole thing, even if you are in the right, is not so weighty that you need call the name of God to witness. Remember that the spectators are, as it were, the judges of the game. If they make any pronouncement, then give in, and don't offer any sign of disapprobation. In this manner the game will be both a delight and the noble education of an honest youth will be pleasing to all.

## The Sixth Law

The sixth law has reference to the length of time of playing. Play until you feel the mind renewed and restored for labour, and the hour for serious business calls you. Who does otherwise seems to do ill. " May you be willing to accept these laws; may you decree their keeping, Romans! " [1]

*Borg., Caban.* " Even as he proposed " (*Sicuti rogavit*).

[1] Vives uses the Roman formula for the passing of laws: " *Velitis, Quirites, jubeatis.*" The response of acceptance being: " *Uti rogas.*"

# XXIII

## CORPUS HOMINIS EXTERIUS—*The Exterior of Man's Body*

DURERIUS PICTOR (the Painter, Dürer), GRYNAEUS, VELIUS

This dialogue has two parts. The former is the Exordium. The second part contains an examination of Dürer's painting. Albert Dürer was a remarkable German painter, whose works are still extant. Simon Grynaeus was renowned by his knowledge of literature, mathematics, and the sacred writings. He taught at Basle, and was married there. Caspar Ursinus Velius was a poet and distinguished historian. He was tutor to the Emperor Maximilian II., as Jovius writes in his *Elogia Doctorum Virorum*.

## I. *Introduction (Exordium)*

*Dürer.* Go away from here, for you will buy nothing, as I know full well, and you only remain in the way, and this keeps buyers from coming nearer.

*Gryn.* Nay, we wish to buy, only we wish you to leave the price to our judgment, and that you should state the limit of time for payment, or, on the other hand, let us settle the time, and you the amount of payment.

*Dürer.* A fine way of doing business! There is no need for me to have nonsense of this sort!

*Gryn.* Whose portrait is this, and what price do you put on it?

*Dürer.* It is the portrait of Scipio Africanus and I price it at four hundred sesterces, or not much less.

## II. *Criticism*

*Gryn.* I pray you, before you favour us with a single word, let us examine the art of the picture. Velius here is half a physicist, and very skilled in knowledge of the human body.

*Dürer.* For some time I have perceived that I was in for being worried by you. Now whilst there are no buyers at hand, you may waste my time as you will.

*Gryn.* Do you call the practical knowledge of your art a waste of time? What would you call that of another's?

*Vel.* First of all you have covered the top of this head with many and straight hairs when the top is called *vertex*, as if a vortex, from the curling round of the hair, as we see in rivers when the water rolls round and round (*convolvit*).

*Dürer.* Stupidly spoken; you don't reflect that it is badly combed, following the custom of his age.

*Vel.* His forehead is unevenly bent.

*Dürer.* As a soldier he had received a wound at the Trebia when he was saving his father.

*Gryn.* Where did you read that?

*Dürer.* In the lost decads of Livy.

*Vel.* The temples are too much swollen.

*Dürer.* Hollow temples would be the sign of madness!

*Vel.* I should like to be able to see the back part of the head.

*Dürer.* Then turn the panel round.

*Gryn.* Why does Cato say amongst his other oracles:

"The forehead is before the back part of the head?"

*Dürer.* How stupid you are! Don't you see in every man the forehead in front of the back part of the head?

*Gryn.* There are some people whose backs I would rather see than their faces!

*Dürer.* And I gladly, *e.g.*, such buyers as you, and soldiers!

*Vel.* Cato was of opinion that the presence of the master was more effective for the oversight of his affairs than his absence. For the rest, why has he such long forelocks?

*Dürer.* Do you speak of these hairs over the forehead?

*Vel.* Yes.

*Dürer.* For many months he had no barber at hand as we have in Spain.

*Vel.* Why have you covered with hair, the hairless part (*glabella*) [1] against its etymology?

*Dürer.* Do you pluck out the hairs with pincers!

*Vel.* The hairs in the nose stand out from the nose. But you, such is your ingenuity, will throw the fault from yourself on to the barber.

*Dürer.* Ignorant that you are! Don't you remember that the customs of those times were harsh, horrible, boorish?

*Vel.* You, too, are ignorant. Have you not read that Scipio was one of the most cultivated and

---

[1] Dr. Bröring renders *glabella*, "the space between the eye-brows." *Glabellus* is derived from *glaber*, the root of which is γλαφ—cf. *scalpo*, to hollow out—*i.e.*, smooth, without hair (Lewis and Short).

polished of all the men of his age, and a lover of what was elegant?

*Dürer.* This painting gives his likeness as he was, when an exile, at Liternum.

*Gryn.* The eyebrows are large, and suitable for Latium; the eyelids too hollow, and the cheeks too much sunk.

*Dürer.* Naturally, from the camp-watches.

*Gryn.* You are not only a painter, but a rhetorician, well versed in turning off any criticism of your work.

*Dürer.* As far as I can see, you are well versed in finding faults.

*Vel.* The picture has the cheeks and lips too much puffed up.

*Dürer.* He is blowing the battle-trumpet.

*Gryn.* And you were blowing on a goblet when you painted this.

*Vel.* On the contrary, he was blowing into a bag made of skin. For elsewhere you have made him hairy, whilst you have scarcely painted any eyelashes.

*Dürer.* They have fallen off by disease.

*Gryn.* What was the disease?

*Dürer.* Seek that from his physician!

*Gryn.* Don't you understand now that you must take off from your price one hundred sesterces for such lack of skill?

*Dürer.* Nay, for your cavils and bothersome questions I ought rather to add two hundred sesterces to the price.

*Vel.* You have made the pupils of the eyes grayish and I have heard that Scipio's were blue.

*Dürer*. And I have heard that his eyes were blue-gray like those of Minerva Bellatrix.

*Vel*. You have made the corners of the eyes too fleshy and the hollows too moist.

*Dürer*. He was weeping because accused by Cato.

*Vel*. The jaws are too long, and the beard very thick and profuse. You would say the hairs are the bristles of swine.

*Dürer*. You are beyond measure, chatterers and talkative cavillers. Get away with you. I won't let you have the opportunity of further criticising the picture.

*Vel*. Please, my Dürer, since you have no other clients, let us go on criticising here.

*Dürer*. What is the good to me?

*Vel*. We will each of us write a distich for you, whereby the picture will be more easily sold.

*Dürer*. My art has no need of your commendation. For skilled buyers who understand pictures, don't buy verses, but works of art.

*Vel*. But your Scipio has his nostrils too much dilated.

*Dürer*. He was in a state of wrath at his accusers.

*Vel*. We see no dimple in his chin.

*Dürer*. It is hidden in his beard. You also don't see his chin nor the double-chin!

*Gryn*. You have saved yourself the trouble of drawing those for the sake of painting a big beard.

*Vel*. The straight and muscular neck pleases me, as also the throat.

*Dürer*. Thank the Lord that you approve of something!

*Vel*. But so that I should not leave something to be

desired in this, I must also say the figure has not sufficient hollow in the throat. When a physiognomist noted this in Socrates, he pronounced it as a sign of slowness of mind. I should wish those shoulders to be a little more erect, and larger.

*Dürer.* He was not so much a fighting soldier as a general. Have you not heard of his apophthegm on the point? When certain soldiers were saying of him, that he was not so valiant a soldier as he was a wise general, he answered: "My mother bore me to be a general, not a soldier." But, depart, if you are not going to be buyers, for I see some tax-farmers approaching.

*Vel.* Let us go for a walk, and let us talk on the way to one another, concerning the human body without considering Scipio, and this portrait. A flat nose does not befit a noble countenance.

*Gryn.* What do you think of the noses of the Huns, then?

*Vel.* Away with such deformities!

*Gryn.* People with turned-up noses are not less deformed. The Persians honoured eagle-nosed people on account of Cyrus, who, they say, had such a shaped nose.

*Vel.* The fore-arm and bend of the arm (*ancon et campe*) are to the arm what the ham of the knee and the knee are to the leg; thence the upper arm (*lacertus*) down to the hand, from the muscles of which also the legs are called muscular (*lacertosa*).

*Gryn.* Is not this the ell (*cubitus*) as used by those who are measuring?

*Vel.* Yes, and *ancon* is another name for it.

*Gryn.* Is not that the way the Roman king came by his name, Ancus?

*Vel.* It was by his curved elbow.

*Gryn.* The hand follows, the chief of all instruments. The hand is divided into fingers, thumb, fore-finger, the middle or disreputable finger, the next to the smallest, and the smallest.

*Vel.* Why has the middle finger a bad name? What crime has it perpetrated?

*Gryn.* Our teacher said that he knew indeed the cause, yet he was not willing to explain it, because it would be unseemly. Don't seek, therefore, to know, for it does not become a well-brought-up youth to inquire into disgraceful matters.

*Vel.* The Greeks named the finger next to the smallest, δακτυλικόν, *i.e.* to say, the ring-finger.

*Gryn.* Clearly so, but on the left, not the right hand, because on it, formerly, they were accustomed to wear rings.

*Vel.* For what reason?

*Gryn.* They say that a vein stretches from the heart to it. If the finger is encircled by a ring it is as if the heart itself is crowned. The knots on the fingers are called knuckles, and this word is used for a knock of the fist. Between the knots are joints and these are called by the general term, joints (*artus*) and knots (*articuli*). It has been handed down to memory, that Tiberius Caesar

had such hard knots that he could bore through
a fresh apple with his fingers.

*Vel.* Have you learned chiromantia?

*Gryn.* I have only heard the name.   What is it?

*Vel.* You would have been able to interpret the lines on
the hands by it.

*Gryn.* I have said I know nothing of it, and so it is.
But if now I were to profess to know something
and looked attentively on your hand, gladly
you would listen willingly to me, and to a man
utterly unskilled in this mode of imposture
you would not altogether refuse your confidence!

*Vel.* How so?

*Gryn.* Because it is the nature of man to listen gladly
to those who profess that they will announce
secret things or what is about to happen.

*Vel.* Why are the Scaevolae so called?

*Gryn.* As if *scaevae;* from *scaea*, which is the left hand.
They say that there are more of the female sex
left-handed than in our sex.

*Vel.* What is *vola?*

*Gryn.* The hollow of the hand in which the lines are.

*Vel.* What does *involare* mean?

*Gryn.* That which you are doing.  Gladly to steal, to
snatch and hide as if in the hollow of the hand,
and as the raving Lucretia did when she
snatched at the eyes of her serving-women.

   [Then follows the Latin for the different
parts of the trunk of the body.]

*Vel.* Do you know the seat of the virtues in the body?

*Gryn.* No; where are they placed?

*Vel.* Modesty in the forehead; in the right hand faithfulness; and sympathy in the knee.

*Gryn.* The sole of the foot is not itself the base of the foot.

*Vel.* So many think.

*Gryn.* Pliny observes that there is a people who make for themselves at mid-day a shadow with the sole of their foot, so great and broad it is! How is it possible?

*Vel.* Clearly the sole in their case reaches from the thigh-bone to the toes.

# XXIV

## EDUCATIO—*Education*

FLEXIBULUS, GRYMPHERANTES, GORGOPAS

The last two dialogues are παραινετικοί or ethical, in the former of which he instructs the boy prince, in the second any one in general.

Flexibulus is a name borrowed from Varro, who uses the word *flexibula* (pliant, flexible). Gorgopas is a name derived from the idea of a stern countenance, such as that of Gorgon is said to have been.   Hence γοργωπὸς, having the eyes or face of Gorgon. Eurip. in *Hercules furens*.   The precepts in this dialogue of Vives are sacred and most wise.   They should be known thoroughly by all sons of princes, for without doubt they would act much better in human affairs if they kept them in view. There are three parts in this dialogue, Exordium, Contentio, and Epilogus.   The Exordium contains the " occasion " and " final cause."

## I. *Introduction* (*Exordium*)

*Flex.* Wherefore did your father send you here to me?

*Grym.* He said that you were a man unusually well instructed, wisely educated, and for that reason well-pleasing to the state.   He desired that I, walking in your steps, might reach a like popularity.

*Flex.* How do you think that you will secure this?

*Grym.* Through the noble education which all say that you have yourself.   My father added that this education would become me better than any other person.

## II. *The Controversy*

*Flex.* Tell me, my boy, how you came to be instructed
　　on this matter by your father?

*Grym.* It was not so much my father who instructed me
　　by his precepts as my uncle, an old man,
　　versed in many things, and long in the counsels
　　of kings.

*Flex.* What then did they teach you, my son and friend?

*Gorg.* Most wise man, look to it that by chance you
　　don't slip through ignorance into some foolish
　　word or deed, or into something boorish, by
　　which you would lose that name of being
　　educated in the best manner.

*Flex.* What! is that name so lightly lost by you?

*Gorg.* Even through single words, with the single bend-
　　ing of the knee, with a single inclination of the
　　head.

*Flex.* Ah! you have matters too delicate and feeble
　　with you—but with us we have much more
　　robust and vigorous standards!

*Gorg.* Our judgments are like our bodies, which can put
　　up with no tripping.

*Flex.* On the contrary, as is easily seen, it is your bodies,
　　rather than your minds, which can bear
　　labour.

*Gorg.* Perhaps you don't know who it is whom you call
　　son and friend.

*Flex.* Are not these honourable names, and full of
　　benevolence?

*Gorg.* Full of benevolence, perhaps, which we don't count
　　much of, but not of dignity and respect, which

we seek as being important. For this gentleman is not accustomed to be called " friend."
And don't you understand that he has the
prefix of " sir " (*domine*) when he is addressed,
and that he has a retinue of varied-coloured
liveried men? Have you not further noticed
that there were so many wax - tapers, so
many badges of honour, so many mourners at
the parental ceremonies of his grandfather's
funeral?

*Flex.* What then? Do you aim at being a lord over
everybody and to have no friends?

*Grym.* So my relations have taught me!

*Flex.* Then may your excellence, my lord (*mi domine*),
present some overwhelming proof of the right
teaching of your relatives!

*Gorg.* You seem to me to sneer at this boy. He is not a
common boy, so don't treat him so!

### Family Teaching

*Grym.* In the first place, they have taught me that I
am of most honourable lineage, which yields
to none in this province, and, on that account,
I must take care diligently, and strive earnestly,
not to degenerate from the rank of my
ancestors; that they have won great honour
to themselves by yielding to no one in position,
dignity, authority, in name, and that I ought
to do the same. If any one should wish to
detract from that honour, immediately I must
fight him. It behoves me to be lavish with
money, and even profuse, but sparing and

frugal in paying honour to others. That it
behoves me, and those like me, by no means
to rise up in the presence of others, nor
to make way for them, nor to let them lead
me, hither and thither, nor to bare the head or
bow the knee to them; not as if any one could
deserve to be shown such honours from me, but
that so I shall conciliate to myself the favour
of men, shall catch the breeze of popularity,
and shall obtain that honour which we always
so greatly have borne in men's mouths and
hearts! It is in this education that the difference exists between those who are nobles, and
those who are not; since the noble has been
rightly accustomed to be educated to excel in
all these matters, whilst the common people
(*ignobiles*), trained to rustic manners, in none
of these things.

*Flex.* And what thinks your excellency, my lord, of
such a method of education?

*Grym.* What indeed! Why, it is by far the highest,
and worthy of my race.

*Flex.* What else then do you seek to learn from me?

*Grym.* In my opinion, nothing further would remain to
be learned, had not my father hurried me
hither to you. My father ordered me, or
rather rigidly enjoined me, to come to you; so
that if there was anything of a more hidden
kind, and more sacred as if of mysteries, by
which I might get more honour for myself,
then that you might, as a favour to him, not
feel it a burden to expound it, that thus our

family, so honourable and exalted, may ascend
still higher, since there are not a few new men
who, relying on their opulence, have come to
light, and seized upon dignities and honours so
that they even dare to vie with the old stand-
ing and honours of our race.

*Flex.* Shameful thing!

*Grym.* Is it not?

*Flex.* This would be visible to a blind man!

*Grym.* Certainly. These new men march about with
a long company of followers, themselves in
gold-decked clothes or clothes of flowered
velvet, or clothes gay as those of Attalus, so that
we seem nothing before them, for we are clothed
in velvet to hide our poverty. If you will
undertake this labour, the reward for thy
labour will be that thou wilt be received by my
father in the number of our family, and wilt be
admitted to his favour and mine, and in process
of time, wilt receive some promotion from us.
Thou wilt always be amongst our clients and,
as it were, under our protection.

*Flex.* What could be a greater reward or more to be
desired? But tell me now, if thou uncoverest
the head or givest way or addressest any one
blandly, why art thou pleasing to them with
whom thou hast dealings?

*Grym.* Just because I meet them in this way.

*Flex.* All these externalities are only the signs which
denote that there is something in the heart,
on account of which they love you, for no one
loves them for themselves.

*Grym.* Why should not everybody love those things
which are of honourable bearing, especially in
my grade of nobility?

*Flex.* Thou hast not yet advanced to that degree that
it should be permitted to thee to say so, and
thou thinkest that thou hast arrived at the
very highest.

*Grym.* I have no necessity to get knowledge and education. My forefathers have left me enough to
live upon. And even if this were lacking, I
should not seek my living by those arts, or by
any means so low, but with the point of the
lance and with drawn sword.

*Flex.* This is high-spirited and fierce, as if indeed
because you are of noble rank you would not
be a man.

*Grym.* Fine words, those!

*Flex.* Which part of you is it that makes you a man!

*Grym.* Myself as a whole.

*Flex.* Is it by your body, in having which you don't
differ from a beast?

*Grym.* By no means.

*Flex.* Not then yourself as a whole, but therefore by
your reason and your mind?

*Grym.* What then?

*Flex.* If, therefore, you permit your mind to be uncultivated and boorish but cherish your body
and take thought for it alone, don't you
transfer yourself from the human, into the
brute, condition? But let us return to the
topic on which we began to speak, for this
digression, if I gave way to it, would lead us a

long way from our purpose. If thou, therefore, yieldest place, and uncoverest thy head,
for what do others take you?

*Grym.* For a noble, nobly instructed and brought
up.

*Flex.* You are too uncouth. Did you hear nothing at
home about the mind, about honesty, about
modesty, and moderation?

*Grym.* In the church, sometimes, I have heard of these
things from preachers.

*Flex.* When those who meet you see what is done by
you, they judge that you are a modest, honest
young man, approving of your actions towards
them, judging modestly and thinking humbly
of yourself. Thence the opinion of benevolence
and graciousness is formed of you.

*Grym.* Please be more explicit.

*Flex.* If people knew that you were so proud that
you looked down on them all with contempt, that you bared your head and bent
your knee to them, not because that honour
was due to them, but because it redounded to
your honour to do it, do you think there would
be any one who would take pleasure in you, or
would love you for your honours sprung from
such false dissimulation?

*Grym.* For why?

*Flex.* Because you do honour to yourself, and take
pleasure in it—not to them. For who will
consider himself indebted to you for that
which you do for your sake? Or shall I
receive your honour not for itself, but as an

outlay which thou offerest for a good opinion
of thyself, not as due to my merits?

*Grym.* So it seems.

### The Teaching of the Better View of Education—Right Government of Oneself

*Flex.* Therefore, benevolence is won if people believe
that honour is paid to *them*, not that *thou*
shouldst be held more courtly and noble.
This will not happen, unless they have the
opinion of thee, that thou esteemest them
higher than thyself and holdest them worthy
of thy honour.

*Grym.* But this does not happen.

*Flex.* If it does not happen, then they must be deceived
on this point, or else thou wilt never obtain
what thou so keenly desirest.

*Grym.* By what way can you persuade me to think so?

*Flex.* Easily. Apply your mind carefully to what I say.

*Grym.* Go on, I beg. For I am sent on this very account
to you, and you shall always be amongst our
*clientèle.*

*Flex.* Ah, that apple is too raw for me!

*Grym.* What do you whisper?

*Flex.* I say the only way will be for you *to be* what you
wish to be thought to be.

*Grym.* How so?

*Flex.* If you wish to make anything warm, do you then
bring it to an imaginary fire?

*Grym.* No, but to a real fire.

*Flex.* If you wish to cleave anything in two, will

you use a picture of a sword depicted on tapestry?

*Grym.* No, an iron sword.

*Flex.* Is there not the same strength with real things as with artificial ones?

*Grym.* Apparently there is a difference.

*Flex.* Nor wilt thou effect the same with a simulated moderation as with real modesty, for falsity at some time or other shows itself for what it is; truth is always the same. In fictitious modesty you say something sometimes or do something, publicly or privately, when you forget yourself (for you are not able always and everywhere to be on your guard), whereby you are caught in your pretences. And as formerly men loved you, since they did not yet know you, afterwards, and for a long time afterwards, they hate you when they have got to know you.

*Grym.* How shall I note this modesty so as to be able to appropriate it as thou teachest?

*Flex.* If thou wilt persuade thyself of what is actually the case, that other people are better than thou art.

*Gorg.* Better indeed! Where are these people? I suppose in Heaven, for on earth there are very few equal; better, no one!

*Grym.* So I have heard often of my father and my uncle.

*Flex.* The circumstance that you do not understand the significance of words leads you far from the knowledge of truth. Tell us, what do you call good, so that we may know if there is a better than thyself?

*Grym.* What do I know of the good? The good comes from being the offspring of good parents.

### *The Real " Good "*

*Flex.* This, therefore, is not yet known to thee, what it is to be good, and yet you talk about what being " better " means. How hast thou reached to the comparative, when as yet thou hast not learned the positive? But how dost thou know that thy forefathers were good? By what mark canst thou make that clear?

*Grym.* What! do you deny that they were good?

*Flex.* I did not know them! How can I then assert anything of their goodness either way? By what method of reasoning canst thou prove that they were good?

*Grym.* Because every one says so of them; but why, I beg, do you ask me all these vexatious questions?

*Flex.* These questions are not vexatious, but necessary, so that thou canst understand what thou art inquiring from me.

*Grym.* Confine your answer, I beg, to a few words.

*Flex.* Many words are necessary to explain that of which you have so crass an ignorance. But since you are so fastidious, I will speak more briefly than the matter, in itself so great, demands to have said of it. Look at me whilst I expound it. Who are the people who are to be called learned? Are they not those who have learning? or are they the rich? or those who have money?

*Grym.* Undoubtedly, those who have learning.

*Flex.* Who, then, are the good? Are they not those who have what is good?

*Grym.* Clearly so.

*Flex* Let us dismiss now the idea of riches, for they are not in themselves really good. If they were, then many people would be found to be better than your father. Merchants and usurers would then surpass honest and wise men in goodness.

*Grym.* Thus it seems, as you say.

### *The Statement of the Problem (Propositio)*

*Flex.* Now, further, weigh what I am about to add in points one by one. Is there not something good in a keen intellect, a wise, mature judgment, whole and sound; in a varied knowledge about all kinds of great and useful affairs; in wisdom; and in carrying into practice these qualities; in determination; in dexterity in pursuing one's business. What do you say of these things?

*Grym.* The very names of these qualities seem to me beautiful and magnificent. So much more are the things themselves great!

*Flex.* Well, then, what shall we say of wisdom, what of religion, piety towards God, to one's country, parents, dependants, of justice, temperance, liberality, magnanimity, equability of mind towards calamity in human affairs, and brave minds in adversity?

*Grym.* These things also are most excellent.

*Flex.* These things alone are *the good* for men.   All the
remaining " goods " which can be mentioned
are common to the good and to the bad, and
therefore are not true " goods."   Observe this,
please, well!

*Grym.* I will do so.


### Assumptio (Hypothesis)—Complexio (Conclusion)

*Flex.* I wish thou wouldst, for thy disposition is not bad,
but is not well cultivated—as yet.   Think now
well over this matter, whether thou possessest
those goods, and, if thou dost, how few thou
hast, and in what slender proportions!   And
if thou examine this question acutely and
subtly, then wilt thou eventually see that
thou art not yet adorned and provided with
goods, great and many, and that no one
amongst the mass of people is less provided
with them than thyself.   For among the multitude are old people, who have seen and heard
much, and persons experienced in most things.
Others there are, devoting themselves to
studies, who sharpen their wits by learning, and
become cultured men; others engage in public
affairs; others occupy themselves with authors,
who will give them the knowledge they want.
Others are industrious fathers of families.
Others follow various arts and excel in them.
Even peasants themselves—how many of the
secrets of nature they possess!   Sailors, too,
know of the course of day and night, the nature

of winds, the position of lands and seas. Some
of the people are holy and religious men, who
serve the Deity with devotion and worship
Him. Others enjoy success with moderation
and bear adversity with bravery. What dost
thou know of these? What energy like theirs
dost thou practise? In what dost thou excel?
In nothing at all except that " No one is better
than me: I am of a good stock." How canst
thou be better, when as yet thou art not *good?*
Neither thy father nor thy relations or ancestors
have been good, unless they had these things
which I have recounted. If they had them,
you can tell. But I doubt it much. You certainly will not be good, unless you become like
those I have described.

*Grym.* You have quite given me a shock, and made me
ashamed. I cannot find anything to even
mutter in reply!

*Gorg.* I have understood none of these things. You
have cast darkness before my eyes.

*Flex.* Naturally. For you came to these considerations
too uncouth, too long infected and enslaved in
contrary opinions. But you are a young man.
How do you think you are going to be classed?
as a master (*dominus*) or as a slave?

*Grym.* As a slave. For if it is as you have expounded,
and I know nothing which seems truer than
what you say, there are very many much
greater and more distinguished than I am, who
are slaves.

*Flex.* Don't be lightly disgusted at what I have said.

Betake yourself home. Alone, think over what I have said. Examine my statements, ponder over them. The more you turn them over in mind, the more you will recognise they are true and certain.

*Grym.* I beseech you proceed, if you yet have further to add, for I feel that at this moment I am a changed man. For the future I shall seem to be another person from my former self.

*Flex.* Would that it may happen to thee as it did to the philosopher Polaemon!

*Grym.* What happened to him?[1]

*Flex.* Owing to a single oration of Xenocrates, from being one of the worst and most incorrigible, he turned out most studious of wisdom and the seeker of every virtue, and was the successor of Xenocrates in the Academy. But thou, my son, now openly hast recognised to how great a degree is lacking in thee the goodness, which others have in an overflowing measure. Now truly, and of thine own good will, thou yieldest place to others and honourest the good in them where thou seest them well furnished, and where thou seest thyself to be deficient. And if thou thus humblest thyself, and seemest to be of slight attainments, thou wilt meet no one for whom thou feelest abject contempt, and whom thy conscience in thy heart does not place before thyself. For thou wilt not be led away to believe any one to be worse than thyself, unless his badness and malice manifest them-

*See Valerius Maximus*, book vi. chap. vi.

selves openly, whilst thine own evil carefully skulks within and is ashamed.

*Grym.* And what follows?

### III. *Epilogue*

*Flex.* If thou doest these things, then wilt thou get the real, solid, noble education itself, and true urbanity; and if, as we are supposing now, thou followest after a courtly life, thou wilt be pleasing to all and dear to all. But even this thou wilt not set at high value, but what will then be the sole care to thee will be, to be acceptable to the Eternal God.

## PRAECEPTA EDUCATIONIS—*The Precepts of Education*

BUDAEUS, GRYMPHERANTES

There are three parts to this dialogue: Exordium, Narratio, and Epilogus.

### I. *Introductory (Exordium)*

*Bud.* What is this so great and so sudden a change in you? It might be included in Ovid's *Metamorphoses*.

*Grym.* Is it a change for the better or the worse?

*Bud.* For the better, in my opinion, at least, if one may argue and estimate as to the goodness of a mind from outward countenance, bearing, words, and actions.

*Grym.* Can you then, my most delightful friend, congratulate me?

*Bud.* I do indeed congratulate you and exhort you to go on, and I pray God and all the saints, that you may have just increase day by day of such fruitfulness. But please don't grudge so dear a friend as I am, to impart the art so distinguished and glorious, which could in so short a time infuse so much virtue in a man's heart.

### II. *The Exposition (Narratio)*

*Grym.* The art and the fountain of this stream is that

very man who is so fruitful in goodness—
Flexibulus, if you know him.

*Bud.* Who does not know the man? He, as I have
heard from my father and my cousins, is a man
of great wisdom and experience of things, not
only known to this city, but also generally
beloved and honoured as only few are. Oh,
fortunate that you are! to have heard him more
closely and to have conversed with him fami-
liarly, and thereby to have gained so great a
fruit in the forming of manliness!

*Grym.* By so much the happier art thou, to have had
all this born with you in your home, as they
tell me, and to be able, not once and again as
I, but every day, as often as you pleased, to
listen to such a father, holding forth wisely on
the greatest and most useful topics.

*Bud.* Stop this, please, and let the conversation proceed,
with which we started, about thee and Flexibulus.

*Grym.* Let us then be silent with regard to your father
since this is your desire: let us return to Flexibulus; nothing is sweeter to me than his discourse, nothing more sagacious than his counsels, nothing more weighty than his precepts,
or more holy. So by this foretaste of himself
which he has provided me, the thirst has been
stimulated and increased in a wonderful degree,
to draw further from that sweet fountain of
wisdom. Those who describe the earth tell us
that the streams are of wonderful formation
and nature; some inebriate, others take away

drunkenness; some send stupor, others sleep. I have experienced that this fountain has the property of making a man of a brute, a useful person of a wastrel, and of a man an angel.

*Bud.* Might I not be able also to draw something from this fountain, though it be with the tip of my lips?

*Grym.* Why shouldst thou not? I will show you the house where he dwells.

*Bud.* Another time! But do thou, whilst we are walking along (or let us sit down, if you like), tell me something of his precepts, those which thou considerest to be his best and most potent.

### The Precepts

*Grym.* I will gladly recall them to memory as far as I am able if it will give you pleasure and be of use. First of all he taught me that no one ought to think highly of himself, but moderately or, more truly, humbly; that this was the solid and special foundation of the best education, and truly of society. Hence to exercise all diligence to cultivate the mind, and to adorn it with the knowledge of things by the knowledge and exercise of virtue. Otherwise, that a man is not a man but as cattle. That one should be interested in sacred matters and regard them with the greatest attention and reverence. Whatsoever on those matters you either hear, or see, to regard it as great, wonder-moving, and as things which surpass your power of comprehension. That you should frequently com-

mend yourself to Christ in prayers, have your
hope and all your trust placed in Him.  That
you should show yourself obedient to parents,
serve them, minister to them and, as each one
has power, be good and useful to them.  That we
should honour and love the teacher even as the
parent, not of our body but (what is greater)
of our mind.  That we should revere the
priests of the Lord, and show ourselves atten-
tive to their teaching, since they are to us in
place of the Apostles and even of the Lord
Himself.  That we should stand up before
the old, uncovering our heads, and attentively
listen to them, from whom, through their long
experience of life, wisdom may be gathered.
That we should honour magistrates, and that
when they order anything we should listen to
what they say—since God has committed us
to their care.  That we should look for, admire,
honour, and wish all good to, men of great ability,
of great learning, and to honest men, and
seek the friendship and intimacy of those from
whom so great fruits can be obtained, and that
we attend to it especially that we turn out like
them.  And in the last place, that reverence is
due to those who are in places of dignity, and
therefore it should be given freely and gladly.
What do you say as to these precepts?

*Bud*. So far as I can form a judgment regarding them,
they are taken out from some rich storehouse
of wisdom.  But tell me if many people do not
come to honour, who don't deserve it, *e.g.*,

priests who don't act in accordance with so great a title, depraved magistrates, and foolish and delirious old men? What is the opinion of Flexibulus of these? Are they to be honoured as greatly as the more capable men?

*Grym.* Flexibulus knew very well that there are many such, but he did not allow that those of my age could judge in matters of this kind. We had not yet obtained such insight and wisdom, that we could judge with regard to them. That forming of opinion in these matters must be left over to wise men, and to those who are placed in authority over us.

*Bud.* Therein he was right, as it seems to me.

*Grym.* He used to add: that a youth ought not to be slow in baring his head, in bending his knee, nor in calling any one by his most honoured titles, nor remiss in pleasant and modest discourse. Nor does it become him to speak much amongst his elders or superiors. For it would not otherwise agree with the reverence due from him. Silent himself, he should listen to them, and drink in wisdom from them, knowledge of varied kinds, and a correct and ready method of speaking. The shortest way to knowledge is diligence in listening. It is the part of a prudent and thoughtful man to form right judgments about things, and in every instance of that about which he clearly knows. Therefore a youth ought not to be tolerated, who speaks hastily and judges hastily, nor one who is inclined to asserting and deciding hastily; that he ought to be reluctant to argue and judge on even small and slight questions of any kind, or, at any rate, rather timid, *i.e.*, conscious of his own ignorance. But if this is true in slight matters, what shall we say of literature, of the branches of knowledge? of the laws of the country, of rites, of the customs and institutions of our ancestors? Concerning these, Flexibulus said, it was not permissible in the youth to urge an opinion or to dispute or to call in question; not to cavil, nor to demand the grounds, but quietly and modestly, to obey them. He supported his opinion by the authority of Plato, a man of great wisdom.

*Bud.* But if the laws are depraved in their morality, unjust, tyrannical?

*Grym.* As to this Flexibulus expressed himself as he had done with regard to old men. " I know full well," said he, " there are many customs in the state which are not suitable, that whilst some laws are sacred, some are unjust, but you are unskilled, inexperienced in the affairs of life, how should you form an opinion? Not as yet have you reached that stage in erudition, in the experience of things, that you should be able to decide. Perchance, such is your ignorance or licence of mind, you would judge those laws to be unjust which are established most righteously and with great wisdom. But who could render manifest those laws which should be abrogated without inquiring, discussing, and deciding on points one by one? For this, you are not yet capable."

*Bud.* That is clearly so. Go on to other points.

### III. *Epilogue*

*Grym.* No ornament is more becoming or pleasing in the youth than modesty. Nothing is more offensive and hateful than impudence. There is great danger to our age from anger. By it we are snatched to disgraceful actions, of which afterwards we are most keenly ashamed. And so we must struggle eagerly against it, until it is entirely overcome, lest it overcome us. The leisurely man, badly occupied, is a stone, a beast; a well-occupied man is in truth a man. Men, by doing nothing, learn to do evil. Food and drink must be measured by the natural desire of hunger and thirst, not by gluttony, and not by brute-lust of stuffing the body. What can be more loathsome to be said than that a man wages war on his own body by eating and drinking, which strip him of his humanity, and hand him over to the beasts, or make him even as it were a log of wood. The expression of the face and the whole body show in what manner the mind within is trained. But from the whole exterior appearance, no mirror of the mind is more certain than the eyes, and so it is fitting that they should be sedate and quiet, not elated nor dejected, neither mobile nor stiff, and that the face itself should not be drawn into severity or ferocity, but into a cheerful and affable cast. Sordidness and obscenity should be far absent from clothing, nurture, intercourse, and speech. Our speech should be neither arrogant nor marked by fear, nor (would he have it by turns) abject and effeminate, but simple and by no means captious; not twisted to misleading interpretations, for if that happens, nothing can be safely spoken, and a noble nature in a man is broken, if his speech is met by foolish and inane cavils. When we are speaking, the hands should not be tossed about, nor the head shaken, nor the side bent, nor the forehead wrinkled, nor the face distorted, nor the feet shuffling. Nothing is viler than lying, nor is anything so abhorrent. Intemperance makes us beasts; lying makes us devils; the truth makes us demigods. Truth is born of God; lying of the Devil, and nothing is so harmful for the communion of life. Much more ought the liar to be shut out from the concourse of men than he who has committed theft, or he who has beaten another, or he who has debased the coinage. For what intercourse in the affairs or business of life or what trustful conversation can there be with the man, who speaks otherwise than as he thinks? With other kinds of vices, this may be possible; but not with lying. Concerning companions and friendship of youths he said much and to the purpose, that this was not a matter of slight moment to the honesty or else the shame of our age, that the manners of

our friends and companions are communicated
to us as if by contagion, and we become almost
such as those are, with whom we have intimate
dealings; and therefore in that matter, there
should be exercised great diligence and care.
Nor did he permit us to seek friendships and
intimacies ourselves, but that they should be
chosen by parents or teachers or educators, and
he taught that we should accept them, and
honour them as they were recommended.   For
parents, in choosing for us, are guided by reason,
whilst we may be seized by some bad desire or
lust of the mind.   But if, by any chance, we
should find ourselves in useless or harmful
circumstances, then it behoves us as soon as
possible to seek advice from our superiors, and
to lay our cares before them.   He said, from
time to time, indeed, very many other weighty
and admirable things, and these things also
he explained with considerable fullness and
exactness.   But these points which I have
already stated were, on the whole, the most
important on the subject of the right
education of youth.

BREDA, IN BRABANT; *the Day of the
Visitation of the Holy Virgin*, 1538.

# INDEX

# Index                                    247